Researching British Military History on the Internet

The British Army and the Armies of the Commonwealth, Empire and Dominions

D1490968

Dr Stuart C Blank

Researching British Military History on the Internet – The British Army and the Armies of the Commonwealth, Empire and Dominions.

First edition March 2007 version 1.0.1

Published by Alwyn Enterprises Ltd,
PO Box 356, Paignton, Devon, TQ3 1WZ, United Kingdom

Copyright © Alwyn Enterprises Ltd 2007

ISBN 0-9554136-0-5 (10 digit version)
ISBN 978-0-9554136-0-5 (13 digit version)

A catalogue record of this book is available from the British Library.

Summary

During the past few years the Internet has become an excellent tool for researching British Military History. The recent advances in computer technology have made the Internet an invaluable tool for discovering data on formations and genealogical (family history) research. Vast amounts of information are now available quickly and easily to the researcher. In short, the Internet is like having the world's biggest library at ones' fingertips. You can access data on units or individuals from anywhere in the world by using your personal computer.

This publication presents some of the best and most well known sites that can be used for "Researching the British Army and the Armies of the Commonwealth, Empire and Dominions". The book does what its title states – it informs the reader of the best sites for researching this enjoyable and engrossing subject.

The operation of internet browsers and e-mail packages are outside the scope of this book - they could be books in themselves. So it is assumed that you can operate an Internet browser and an e-mail package. This document indicates where you can find informative internet sites. This data will benefit your military research and by doing this it will give significant added value to your research activities.

Some of the topics covered in this book are:

- Napoleonic battles
- Victorian Campaigns
- World War 1
- World War 2
- Military Museums
- Archive Facilities
- Medals Research

- British Regiments, units and Formations
- Regimental Associations
- Military Intelligence
- Organisations for Veterans
- Monuments, Graves and Rolls of Honour

The Appendices give information on Regimental Histories, Associations and museum collections. A brief overview of battles and campaigns of the British Army is available in Appendix D whilst Appendix A gives details of popular search engines.

Researching British Military History on the Internet
The British Army and the Armies of the Commonwealth, Empire and Dominions

Contents

Abbreviations & Notation

ABF	Army Benevolent Fund
ADSL	This is a type of wire (land) based telephone line that allows the fast transfer of data over the Internet. Typically speaking, it may allow downloaded transfer rates of up to 8Mbytes.
AIF	Australian Imperial Forces
AJEX	Association of Jewish Ex-Servicemen
AMF	Australian Military Forces
ANZAC	Australian and New Zealand Army Corps
APAC	Asia, Pacific and African Collections. This Department at the British Library includes the India Office Records (OIOC).
ASAC	Armed Services Assistance Centre, Australia
BACSA	British Association for Cemeteries in South Asia
BL	British Library
BSC	British Security Coordination
CBF	Canadian Battlefields Foundation
CEF	Canadian Expeditionary Force
CIA	Central Intelligence Agency (USA)
CMHG	Canadian Military History Gateway
COI	Co-ordinator of Information (1940 – 41). The forerunner of the USA's OSS.
Comms	Communications
CWGC	Commonwealth War Graves Commission
DND	Department of National Defence (Canadian)
EIC	East India Company
FANY	First Aid Nursing Yeomanry. Now called Princess Royals' Volunteer Corps (PRVC)
FBI	Federal Bureau of Investigation (USA)
GC	George Cross
GWA	Great War Association
HEIC	Honourable East India Company
HR	Human Resources
HTML	Hyper Text Mark-up Language - the language used for writing web pages.
ISP	Internet Service Provider
IT	Information Technology
IWM	Imperial War Museum, London, United Kingdom
LI	Light Infantry
MGC	Machine Gun Corps
MI6	Military Intelligence Department 6. Its official title is the Secret Intelligence Service.
MVPA	Military Vehicle Preservation Association
NAS	National Archives of Scotland
NASA	National Archives of South Africa

NCO	Non-commissioned officer
NFFCA	National Federation of Far Eastern Prisoner of War Clubs and Associations
NZ	New Zealand
NZDF	New Zealand Defence Force
NZMHS	New Zealand Military Historical Society
OBLI	Oxfordshire and Buckinghamshire Light Infantry
OMRS	Orders and Medals Research Society
OSS	Office of Strategic Services (created June 1942). The forerunner of the USA's Central Intelligence Agency.
OWI	Office of War Information. A USA agency which reported to the President of the USA.
POW	Prisoner of War
PRO	Public Record Office (London, United Kingdom). Now called The National Archives (TNA).
PRONI	Public Record Office Northern Ireland
PRVC	Princess Royals' Volunteer Corps
RAF	Royal Air Force
RCMP	Royal Canadian Mounted Police
RFC	Royal Flying Corps. A predecessor formation to the Royal Air Force
RN	Royal Navy
RNAS	Royal Naval Air Service
RSA	Returned and Services Association (New Zealand)
SAC	South African Constabulary
SCLI	Somerset and Cornwall Light Infantry
SIS	Secret Intelligence Service (also known as MI6 – see above)
SOE	Special Operations Executive
SSAFA	Soldiers', Sailors', Airmen and Families Association
STS	Special Training School
SVC	Singapore Volunteer Corps
TNA	The National Archives, London, United Kingdom
UK	United Kingdom
URL	Uniform Resource Locators (The address of a website)
USA	United States of America
VC	Victoria Cross
VMS	Victorian Military Society
VVAA	Vietnam Veterans Association of Australia
WFA	Western Front Association
WRAC	Women's Royal Army Corps
WW1 / WW2	World War One (1914 – 1919) / Two (1939 – 1945)

1 Introduction to the Internet

The Internet (also called the "World Wide Web" or "net") has become an important tool for those seeking information on military history. It is international in nature and people from outside the UK can contact British organisations easily and relatively quickly. Increasingly, more websites are being added to the Internet and it is an excellent medium for contacting those with whom you share a common interest, in say a Regiment or campaign.

This book does not aim to teach you about the technicalities of the Internet but it does intend to show you how to use the web as a vital research tool. It assumes you are familiar with the fundamentals of operating a computer - that you know how to operate an Internet browser and e-mail software. Its true aim is to help you get the most out of the Internet when researching the British Army and its associated formations.

1.1 What is the Internet?

The Internet is a system of inter-connected computers upon which information is stored. Most home users connect to the Internet via an Internet Service Provider (ISP). They usually do this over a telephone line using a modem via either a dial-up connection (with transfer rates of about 54 Kbytes) or high-speed connections such as ADSL. ADSL offers faster download rates (up to 8 Mbytes) so the user spends less time waiting for web pages to load. In recent years, there has been a migration from dial-up services (at 54 Kbytes) to broadband (at various faster rates). The latter is getting more and more popular and is now becoming the norm.

These inter-connected computers store pages of information which may contain text, graphics such as charts and images (including photographs), sound or even video clips. Unfortunately there is no complete reference system to the Internet - there are pages being added and deleted continuously. The Internet is vast and only a small portion has been indexed. You can compare it to a large library for which there is no index. To overcome this un-indexed state two sorts of internet site have evolved and they are called search engines and directory listings.

These search engines and directories list and catalogue most of the major internet sites. You can use these directories / search engines to start a search for a particular topic. Often a website dealing with a specific issue might have links to other websites that you can then follow.

When a computer undertakes a search it cannot distinguish between very useful sites and ones that contain little useful information. Often the search engine will look for a specific word or words so if you search for "Scottish Regiments" it may not find Regiments listed under the British Army or the Scottish Guards. Computers do not posses intelligence like humans - they simply look for what was specified. However, search engines have tried to overcome this disadvantage and now they often have a relevance rating for the "hits" found after conducting a search. We will discuss search engines in more detail later and how to get the best from them.

1.2   Electronic Mail

Another excellent tool which proves invaluable whilst conducting research is called "e-mail" or electronic mail. E-mail is essentially a "letter" in text form (some e-mail packages use HTML the language of web pages) sent via a computer. If you think of writing a letter and then posting it, the e-mail comparison is using a computer to write the letter and an Internet connection for posting it. The only drawback is that the recipient must have an e-mail or website address.

Is there a directory of e-mail addresses?
The answer to that question is that there is no such thing as the "phone book" or "yellow pages" with everyone's e-mail address. The analogy is that most people are ex-directory. However, museums, archive facilities and societies etc will often gladly give out their e-mail and website addresses. Nowadays, they are usually on any stationary received from an organisation or even individuals.

How do I find information on the Internet?
There is not one best way to retrieve information from the Internet. The way of searching can depend upon personal preferences or a trial and error approach. However, two useful methods and the ones recommended are search engines and directories.

1.3   Search Engines

There is a multitude of search engines and these sites perform the indexing of the web. A search engine is a piece of software that searches the internet for sites dealing with or mentioning a particular topic or issue. Different search engines use different methods of searching. A selection of the most popular search engines is given in Appendix A.

Some, but not all, search engines ask the owner(s) of a website(s) to submit the site for indexing. The person submitting the site has to describe or give keywords about the site. Sometimes it is the text / keywords used by the person who submitted the site that is searched. Thus, the specified keywords / text are very important as they are used to indicate hits (occurrences) created by the searching mechanism. Other search engines trawl through the pages on various websites related to the query and they order the sites based on the frequency of occurrence of the search text.

Search engines look for particular words that you enter in a text box. You can have different logic applied to the words you type at the prompt e.g.

Searching for   "British Regiments"
Search Text: "British Regiments"

Results could list those sites with word combinations:

2

"British" OR "Regiments"
"British" AND "Regiments"
Exact phrase match "British Regiments"

You will get different results depending on the search engine you use (see Table 1). It can be seen, that the number of hits for "British OR Regiments" is much larger than those for "British AND Regiments". This is the same for Altavista, Google and Yahoo. Lycos only allows a Boolean AND search so the hits for both searches are equal.

Table 1 Internet Search for "British Regiments"

Search	Search Engine	Results
British OR Regiments	www.altavista.com	470,000,000 hits
	www.google.co.uk	142,000,000 hits
	www.lycos.com[1]	259,900 hits
	http://uk.yahoo.com	463,000,000 hits
British AND Regiments	www.altavista.com	3,680,000 hits
	www.google.co.uk	495,000 hits
	www.lycos.com	259,900 hits
	http://uk.yahoo.com	3,720,000 hits

Most of the default searches are all based upon the full text (i.e. an AND search) entered into the search box. More complex searches can be performed and these can normally be conducted by finding an "Advanced Search" link. Once in the Advanced Search area you can specify the various words and logic for your search. It is recommended that you consider using the Advanced Search criteria as this reduces the number of hits and makes it easier to manage the results of the search.

1.4   Directories

An alternative to searching for a set of words is to use a directory. A directory is a category based listing of websites. They are generally based on a tree like structure. First you identify the top level and then work down each of the sub-levels until the lowest level related to the issue is found.

Yahoo is one portal that has a directory (see *http://uk.dir.yahoo.com*) as well as the ability to search the Internet. The initial issue is to identify the main category such as "History" and then to follow links to "Military History" and the period of interest e.g. "World War 2"

An *example* based upon finding information on the Battle of Dunkirk is:

Directory > Arts > Humanities > By Time Period > 20th Century > Military History > World War II > Battles and Campaigns > European Theatre > Battle of Dunkirk

---

[1] Lycos only allowed a Boolean AND search. There was no facility for the OR search.

Each of the ">" indicates a sub-category of the item preceding the ">". It can be realised that there is a huge number of permutations based on cross-references and by following the directory's tree based structure.

Generally the top level of a directory is located on the home page of a particular site. It may be necessary to look for the word "Directory" (perhaps via the sitemap of the search engine) or it may be more obvious. Directories are very useful for finding lists of sites devoted to a particular topic. They are not however good for finding individual pages concerning a topic. Directories may only list a particular site under one heading so in order to find a specific site it may be necessary to make use of the search facility on the directory page.

1.5   Discussion Groups and Mailing Lists

Basically discussion groups and mailing lists function in a similar manner. A discussion group is either a webpage or an e-mail based system where topics related to a central theme are raised and answered. The webpage versions are often organised in a manner such that clicking on a message opens the message to display its contents or a tree structure with sub-branches are shown. The e-mail version of discussion groups / mailing lists function like normal e-mail and the group's correspondence is forwarded to your specified e-mail address. Reponses are usually directed to a central e-mail address to which all members of the list subscribe to.

2 Sites for Regiments, Units and Formations

In this section we consider websites that cover a spectrum of Regiments, Organisations or Formations. Most Regiments are now migrating towards having an internet site and to catalogue them all would be a huge task. We consider here those sites that provide links to individual regiments or units.

The main Army website (*www.army.mod.uk*) is trying to act as a central hub for regimental sites. Instead of reviewing each and every site a selection of regimental / formation websites are listed in Appendix C. Regiments often have a strong sense of camaraderie and ex-members often keep in touch with the Regiment in which they served.

2.1 The British Army
www.army.mod.uk
This is a huge site and it is the government's official internet site for the British Army. The main divisions on the site are: (1) the Serving Soldier, (2) Welfare and Family matters, (3) Careers, (4) News, (5) Units, (6) Deployments, (7) Ceremonial, (8) Museums, (9) Equipment, (10) Sports, and a (11) What's New section.

Brief introductions to these segments on the British Army website are below. It is not possible to cover all the issues and topics on the website and these comments are to serve as introductory notes.
(1) Serving Soldier
The Serving Soldier section has information useful to those currently serving like career guidance, welfare, terms and conditions of employment and money matters etc.
(2) Welfare and Family
This part of the site contains material relating to postings, family support, post service aftercare, support for soldiers, agencies that can help, casualty and compassionate issues and "A What's" happening link.
(3) Careers
This presents information regarding the careers in the Regular Army and Territorial Army. The page has links to combat troops, engineering, IT / Comms, Logistics, Healthcare, HR / Admin & Finance, specialist units and Educational careers. There is a lot of data on what service life is like and it makes interesting reading.
(4) News
This section provides information on the latest events of significance to the Army or the Army way of life.
(5) Units
The Army is a large organisation and like all its counterparts it has many sections, units and departments (see www.army.mod.uk/unitsandorgs/index.htm). The Army classifies its structure under:

- Major Headquarters
- Divisions and Brigades
- Specialist Units
- Arms and Services
- Regiments and Battalions

- Training Establishments
- Agencies
- Cadets and
- Territorial Army

There is information on a large number of these branches of the Army and their sub-departments. The scope is vast and it is not possible to detail them all here.

(6) Deployments
The Army is currently deployed in over 80 countries around the world. Some deployments may be fully operational and others are only single military advisors. This page gives a list of the main deployments and links to pages which contain more details.

(7) Ceremonial
The main ceremonial duties of the British Army are the Edinburgh Tattoo, Beating the Retreat, Remembrance Sunday, the Queen's Guard (outside Buckingham Palace), the Queen's Life Guard (the Horse Guards in Whitehall), Trooping The Colour, the State Opening of Parliament and State Visits. The website gives further details of all of these wonderful military spectaculars.

(8) Museums
The main page for this section presents links to:

- The National Army Museum (reviewed in Section 8.1),
- The Army Museums Ogilby Trust (in Section 8.3),

(9) Equipment
The equipment used by the British Army is revealed here in detail. The range of equipment covers individual equipment, small arms and support weapons, armoured fighting vehicles, artillery and air defence, engineering equipment, logistical vehicles, the electronic battlefield, army aircraft, landing and assault boats and nuclear, biological and chemical defence systems.

(10) Sport
Physical fitness is an important part of a soldiers' life. To this end the Army promotes physical exercise and this part of the Army's website gives details of sports and activities available to serving soldiers of the British Army.

(11) What's New
Like its header, this section informs the reader what has happened recently.

2.2   British and Commonwealth 'Regiments.Org'

www.regiments.org
This is one of the best sites on the Internet regarding the formations of the British and Commonwealth Armies. It is a superb site and contains lots of useful information. The focus of the site is the history of the Regiments of all of the territories and successor states that were part of the British Empire or Commonwealth. In the sections devoted to individual regimentals there are unit and

battalion histories, lists of data for such things as deployments, details of books on specific regiments and sometimes bibliographies. This data is complemented by extensive cataloguing of related external sites for each regiment.

The emphasis is upon the British Regimental system. Some countries like Canada have continued with that system whilst others, such as Iraq, have not continued these traditions. The regiments are listed under their nations. There is data on the campaigns / wars in which each regiment fought and their Battle Honours.

The same sort of framework or layout has been used for each regiment. Each of the individual regimental pages contains data regarding:

- title changes and lineage
- battalion's service histories
- campaigns and wars in which the regiment was involved
- battle honours
- badges

- list of colonels
- alliances
- bibliographies
- links to external sites specialising in the regiment under consideration

There are indexes of all the regiments of the Empire and the Commonwealth nations. Regional and national indexes contain the most common title variations and these are linked to the individual regiment's dedicated pages. There is also data on the precedence of regiments.

It is worth noting that this site does not cover (1) naval or air forces except their most notable land forces such as the Royal Marines and the RAF Regiment, (2) enemy forces, (3) there is no data on Mozambique's forces as they have never been linked to the British army (However Mozambique is part of the Commonwealth), (4) forces of the USA unless they can be traced prior to Independence in 1783, (5) biographical data with the exceptions of Royalty's military careers, colonels of regiments / commanders of large formations and external biographical links regarding the conduct of wars or history or regiments.

2.3   The Regimental War Path 1914 – 1918
http://warpath.orbat.com
Listed on this site are the regiments from Britain and the Commonwealth that were involved in the Great War. The site is organised by country or geographical region and covers formations from:

- Australia – mounted regiments, infantry battalions and divisions
- New Zealand – mounted and infantry regiments, Royal New Zealand Artillery and divisions.

- Canadian – mounted and infantry regiments and divisions,
- East Africa – divisions
- South Africa – no formations listed yet

- Britain – cavalry, yeomanry and infantry regiments, the Royal Artillery, divisions and miscellaneous units.
- West Africa – no formations listed yet.
- India – divisions.

2.4   The Royal Artillery 1939 – 1945

www.ra39-45.pwp.blueyonder.co.uk

During the Second World War the Royal Regiment of Artillery expanded not only in size but scope as well. The war caused the creation of new branches for Anti-tank, Anti-aircraft duties and the Regiment also took on a proliferation of other roles.

At the end of the war, in 1945, the Regiment represented about two-fifths of the entire British Army or about 700,000 men. The scope of the Regiment's activities during the war covered not only traditional artillery roles and those mentioned above but members of the Regiment also undertook flying spotter planes, parachuting and being glider based troops. At sea, they manned the guns of armed merchantmen and on land they built roads, landing strips etc and fought as infantry.

The principal aim of this website is to record as much about the activities of the Regiment in World War 2. At the time of writing, this website does an admirable job at recording the activities of the Regiment and it is an excellent reference point from which to start research into the Royal Artillery.

2.5   Irish Soldiers

www.irishsoldiers.com

This site is organised and run by the Military Heritage of Ireland Trust. The main objective of the Trust is to encourage and facilitate research into the military history of Ireland. It must be remembered that Irish personnel served in both Irish (Eire) Regiments and British Regiments. This site is an excellent gateway to other sites dealing with Irish military history – there are links to sites for:

- Conflict in Ireland
- The Williamite Wars
- The 1798 Rebellion
- The Twentieth Century

Links to details of Irish personnel serving in British, Canadian, South African and American forces are given and they make interesting reading.

2.6   New Zealand Defence Forces 1860 – 1883

www.atonz.com/genealogy/nzdefence.html

This private website deals with a little known issue – that of the NZ Defence Force in the nineteenth century. After the outbreak of the Anglo Maori War in 1860 the NZ Government decided to raise its own local force.

In 1864 the Government's policy was to be militarily self-reliant. Reliance would no longer be put on Crown forces but local forces and Maori auxiliaries. This site tells their fascinating story.

2.7   Canadian Military History Gateway
www.cmhg.gc.ca
The Canadian Military History Gateway (CMHG) is an internet based service providing access to websites and digitised resources about the military history of Canada. The site was developed by the Department of National Defence (DND) as an initiative supported by the National Defence On-Line programme and the Department of Canadian Heritage's Canadian Culture Online Program. The CMHG aims to provide free access to Canadian military history museums, libraries, archival facilities and other heritage organisations.

2.8   Indian Military History
Before Independence (in 1947) the Indian Military was primarily run by European officers and non-commissioned officers. The Government of India was essentially administered by the British through the India Office and the history of the Indian armed forces dates back to the days of the Honourable East India Company (HEIC). The following websites consider the (British Administered) Indian Military and they are very useful for conducting genealogical research and / or studies of (Indian) units and formations.

2.8.1   Military Family History in India
http://members.ozemail.com.au/~clday/
This website is ideal for those interested in tracing their British, European and Anglo-Indian military family history. Although called "Indian" it encompasses the modern day India, Burma, Pakistan and Bangladesh. Of particular interest to the military historian are: (1) Regimental histories covering units posted to India and (2) Military records.

The latter (2) covers:

- Officers of the Madras Regt (1758 – 1958)
- Military & civilian personnel at the Siege of Lucknow (1857)
- Recipients of the Indian Mutiny Medal (1859)
- Officers of the Bengal Army of Foreign Nationality (1758 – 1834)
- Army medical, veterinary and ecclesiastical officers
- Madras Staff Corp Officers (1873)
- Officers of Bengal, Madras & Bombay Regt (101st to 106th Foot) (1873)

Also the site helps to trace the British Army in India as there is data on:

- Muster Lists for the Scots Brigade (1804)
- British Army Pensioners in India (1800 – 1857)
- British Army casualty list for the 2nd Afghan War (1878 – 1880)
- Adjutant's Roll for Duke of Cornwall's Light Infantry (1888) and their married roll (1889)

2.8.2   For the King-Emperor
www.king-emperor.com

This website specialises in the "Indian Army on Campaign during the Edwardian and Georgian Eras 1901 – 1939". The Indian Army has no parallel in history. In its early beginning, during the seventeenth century, it was part of a private army of the East India Company. Eventually, it became the second largest fighting force in the British Empire.

During World War 1 the Indian Army sent hundreds of thousands of soldiers to the battlefields of Flanders, France, Gallipoli, Salonika, East Africa and The North West Frontier. Indian troops also served in the Middle Eastern campaigns such as Egypt, Palestine, Mesopotamia and Persia. When the Great War ended the Indian Army had an excellent service record. During the inter-war years the Indian Army looked after the Frontiers of India and continued the traditions of their strong esprit de corps.

The website gives details of some officers and men, medals for the various campaigns and articles on the Indian Army. It is an interesting site and one of very few which consider the Indian Army whilst it was part of the British Empire.

2.9   Australian and New Zealand Army Corps (ANZAC)
www.anzacs.net

There is an enormous amount of information on ANZAC formations at this website. The names and details of the 3219 fallen soldiers buried in 28 cemeteries plus the 6393 on memorials at Gallipoli are detailed here.

The histories of the ANZAC formations are given and the site indicates that Australia, at the start of the Great War initially pledged 20,000 troops to help the Allied war effort. At the time New Zealand already had conscription and they also pledged troops. The Australian & NZ forces were assembled together in October 1914 and the name ANZAC was born.

2.10   Community Based Formations

These websites are themed on "communities". During the Great War (WW1) men from a specific region or locality often enlisted en-masse. They all originated from a particular city, town or district and served together. After the battlefield slaughters of various regional units the policy of having community units was stopped because the male portion of a district or town was decimated and whole communities suffered after just one battle.

2.10.1 The Accrington Pals

www.pals.org.uk

This website is dedicated to the memory of the 11th (Service) Battalion (Accrington) East Lancashire Regiment. This unit is better known as the "Accrington Pals". The Accrington Pals is probably the best known British battalion of the First World War. The formation was created in the early months of WW1 just after Kitchener's famous call for a volunteer army.

Groups of friends from all walks of life who lived near Accrington enlisted and formed the new battalion. On the opening day of the battle of the Somme (1st July 1916), the Pals went over the top and suffered devastating losses. The losses were very hard to bear in a community where everyone had a relative in the battalion. They all suffered a killed or wounded relative. Although the battalion was reformed it had lost its Pals character and so had the British Army.

2.10.2 The Leeds Pals

www.leedspals.co.uk

This is the story of the 15th (Service) Battalion of the West Yorkshire Regiment in the First World War. They responded like many others to Kitchener's Call to Arms and the Battalion was raised. The general idea was that the Pals Battalions would consist of friends, relatives, workmates and colleagues and this would give the unit a strong cohesive force. To be accepted they had to pass rigorous requirements relating to education, intelligence and medical issues.

By the 8th September 1914 the Battalion was 1,275 men strong. This was considered to be the complete set of "Leeds Pals" but their number eventually rose to approximately 2,000. Of the 900 Leeds Pals who went 'over the top' on the first day of the Battle of the Somme 750 were killed. Leeds was yet another city whose young men were decimated on that fateful day.

2.10.3 The Birmingham Pals

www.birminghampals.co.uk

This website is about the history of the "Birmingham Pals". More specifically it considers the three Birmingham Battalions which served in the Great War. They were the 14th, 15th and 16th Royal Warwickshire Regiment.

2.10.4 Scottish Footballers in the Great War

www.geocities.com/athens/pantheon/3828/

This is an unusual site and certainly the only one the author knows about dealing with footballers who fought in the Great War. The site is a memorial to the players of the Heart of Midlothian Football Club who enlisted en-masse in the British Army during November 1914. It was the first football club to do so and shortly afterwards other players from other clubs followed suit. They are also commemorated on this unusual site.

2.10.5 The Thin Blue Line
www.thinblueline.org.uk
The men from the Sussex Police Forces who enlisted and served in the Great War are commemorated here. The Police Forces covered are Brighton, East Sussex, Eastbourne, Guildford, Hastings, Hove, Reigate, Surrey and West Sussex.

2.11 British Light Infantry Regiments
www.lightinfantry.org.uk
The Light Infantry has earned a splendid reputation since its formation in 1968. A new era dawns with the formation of "The Rifles" on 7th February 2007 and it will be more important than ever to preserve the memory and heritage of the Light Infantry and its predecessor regiments.

This site holds data on the following Light Infantry (LI) formations: the Light Infantry, 6th Battalion The (Somerset and Cornwall) Light Infantry (Volunteers), County LI (covering various LI units), the Duke of Cornwall's, Durham, Royal Guernsey, Hereford, Highland, Royal Jersey, King's Own Yorkshire, King's Shropshire, Oxfordshire & Buckinghamshire, Royal Marine, Somerset, Perthshire, Donegal, Band of the Light Division, 43rd Wessex Association, Somerset & Cornwall, Devonshire & Dorset, Royal Gloucestershire, and the Berkshire and Wiltshire.

2.12 Somerset & Cornwall Light Infantry
(6 Oct 1959 – 10 Jul 1968)
www.scli.co.uk
The SCLI was formed on the 6th Oct 1959, by the amalgamation of the Somerset LI (Prince Albert's) and the Duke of Cornwall's LI. This website covers the SCLI's history, acts as a repository for online memoirs and a forum for the Regiment. Subjects covered are battle honours, colours, insignia & medals, Regimental chapels, the Light Infantry band and a timeline of the Regiment etc.

3   Wars, Battles and Campaigns and Related Associations

3.1   *Cromwell 400*

www.lib.cam.ac.uk/exhibitions/Cromwell/
Oliver Cromwell was born in Huntingdon on the 25th April 1599. This website
provides an opportunity to highlight the significance of this famous man. Cromwell
was born into a wealthy family and he was educated at Huntingdon grammar school
and later at Cambridge University. He made his living by farming and collecting
rents. His income was modest and he found himself supporting a large family – his
widowed mother, wife and eight children.

Cromwell came to the forefront after the Civil war broke out in the summer of 1642.
Initially he was a captain of a small body of mounted troops. Later, he was promoted
to colonel and given command of a cavalry regiment. His military successes grew
and grew until he was the second in command of the newly formed parliamentary
army. His military standing gave him enhanced political power and in December
1653 he became the Lord Protector. Through this office he shared political power
with parliament and a council. He remained in this office until his death in 1658 and
this website provides an interesting insight into this man and his achievements.

3.2   *The Cromwell Association*

www.olivercromwell.org and www.cromwellcollection.org.uk
Oliver Cromwell became famous during the English Civil War. Since his death in
1658 as Lord Protector his life, ambitions, motives and actions have been the subject
of scholarly investigation and debate. The Cromwell Association was founded in
1935 to commemorate Oliver Cromwell (1599 – 1658), and to stimulate interest in
Cromwell and the general history of the British Isles from the date of his birth until
the Restoration. In addition, the Association aims to encourage the study of
Cromwell and the history of this period which includes the Civil War, the
Commonwealth and the Protectorate.

The Association seeks to achieve these aims via commissioning plaques and
memorials, holding meetings, holding day-schools, publishing news / information
about the period, working with the Cromwell Collection and generally promoting
this period in history.

The Cromwell Collection is located at the Huntingdon Library (in The County
Record Office, Huntingdon, England). It is sponsored by the Cromwell Association
and the Collection is a comprehensive collection of materials regarding Cromwell.
The Collection is freely available to all and it is hoped that the Collection will
become popular with students who are studying this fascinating period. The
catalogue of the Collection includes details of the original documents as well as
secondary sources such as books in its library.

3.3 The English Civil Wars

http://easyweb.easynet.co.uk/~crossby/ECW/index.htm
This smallish site aims to introduce the reader to the English Civil War. It has sections on the technology, tactics, people, events and battles. There are also details of re-enactment groups who specialise in this era.

The site was written by the University of Aberystwyth's "Education on the Internet" course and the material was designed as a reference source for the Key Stage 3 History qualification.

3.4 English Civil War Publications

www.lukehistory.com/resources/index.html
This site is collating digital images of publications dating from the civil war. Publications being added to the site include:

- His Majesties Declaration to the Ministers, Freeholders, Farmers and substantial copyholders of the County of York – this is the proclamation that summed up the King's position just before raising his standard.
- The Kings Majesties Alarum for Open War – this decries the King's plans to fight
- England's Oaths – a pamphlet with oaths of allegiance.
- True and Happy Newes from Worcester – an account of the Battle of Powick Bridge (Sept 1642)

Also, there are religious publications, papers on the Thirty Years' War and Blackletter Ballads at this site.

3.5 French and Indian War

http://en.wikipedia.org/wiki/French_and_Indian_War
The "French and Indian War" is the American name for the decisive conflict that occurred during 1754 to 1763 in North America. The antagonists were the Kingdoms of Great Britain and France. The War resulted in France losing all of its possessions in North America except for some Caribbean Islands and two small islands near Newfoundland. The British acquired Canada and Spain got Louisiana in compensation for the loss of Florida to the British.

3.6 American Revolutionary War

http://en.wikipedia.org/wiki/American_Revolutionary_War
The American Revolutionary War (1775–1783) is also known as the "American War of Independence". This war was fought between Great Britain and the thirteen British colonies in North America. The war erupted largely as a result of the economic policies of the British government. Other nations became involved, including the French, Spanish and the Dutch. They all fought the British and numerous American Indians joined both sides of the conflict.

The British were able to utilise their naval superiority and they often had control of the coastal cities but the countryside eluded them. The involvement of the French proved critical and eventually the British lost.

3.7   AmericanRevolution.org
www.americanrevolution.org/britisharmy.html
The main site (*www.americanrevolution.org*) deals with the American War of Independence. This campaign was fought between the Loyalists and the Colonialists. The British and the Colonialists were the main combatants. Associate Professor E E Curtis of Wellesley College (Yale University, USA) has written an excellent review of the "Organisation of the British Army in the American Revolution" and it is included on this website. If you are interested in this war then this is an essential site for you to visit.

3.8   Napoleonic Wars
http://en.wikipedia.org/wiki/Napoleonic_Wars
The Napoleonic Wars were a series of wars fought during Napoleon Bonaparte's rule of France. These wars revolutionised the doctrine of European army and artillery systems. The French were leaders in the new doctrines and they rose to power. There is no consensus as to when the Napoleonic Wars started and the conflicts sparked by the French Revolution ended.

This site is informative and is an excellent introduction into the subject. There are details of the First to the Seventh Coalitions and issues such as the Gunboat Wars. If you are researching the Napoleonic wars then this is a useful site from which to start.

3.9   Napoleonic Guide
www.napoleonguide.com
The Napoleonic Guide is the perfect reference for everything relating to the life and times of the famous French Emperor Napoleon Bonaparte. Although this site deals with Napoleon, it does have a wealth of information on the British forces that fought against Napoleon and its main focus is the period between 1796 and 1815.

The site covers both land battles and sea engagements. However, the latter are out of the scope for this publication. Napoleon's military career included conquering most of Europe and he was a feared leader. The following military campaigns are covered in details on the site:

a) The First Coalition 1792–1797. In this period most of Europe was united against the revolutionary French forces. Battles in this period covered Valmy, Jemappes, and Toulon which catapulted Napoleon towards power.
b) Egypt Adventure 1798–1801. In response to British interests in India, Napoleon launched an invasion of Egypt. When British Admiral Nelson destroyed Napoleon's

fleet at the Battle of the Nile he became marooned in Egypt.

c) The Second Coalition 1798–1801. This period deals with Napoleon's expedition to Egypt, and clashes in North Italy, Germany and Switzerland. There are descriptions of battles for the Pyramids, Marengo and Hohenlinden.

d) The Third Coalition 1805. This covers the surrender at Ulm and the crushing victory of Austerlitz.

e) The Fourth Coalition 1806–1807. In 1806 the attack on Prussia occurred and Napoleon defeated his enemies at Jena and Auerstadt. Also included are details on the Battle of Eylau.

f) The Fifth Coalition 1809. This covers the campaigns in the Peninsula, Danube and battles at Aspern-Essling and Wagram.

g) The Peninsular War 1808–1814. The Peninsular War bled Napoleon's army of its finest troops. The battles involved included those with the Duke of Wellington at Talavera, Rolica, Vimiero and Salamanca.

h) The Russian Campaign 1812. This was a major blunder. The march on Moscow and the battle of Borodino are considered.

i) The Liberation of Germany 1813. This includes the action at Dresden and the battle of nations at Leipzig.

j) France Invaded During 1814. The 1814 invasion by Napoleon's enemies into his France saw him outnumbered and encircled.

k) The 100 Days 1815. This is the famous Waterloo Campaign which decided the fate of modern Europe.

l) The War of 1812–1815. The war of 1812 was a "sideshow" but it decided the fate of modern Canada and the USA.

m) The West Indies 1793–1810. The battles for the West Indies were bloody and lengthy. The slave revolt of San Domingo, Toussaint and l'Ouverture are included.

3.10 First Anglo-Afghan War
http://en.wikipedia.org/wiki/First_Anglo-Afghan_War

This war lasted from 1839 to 1842. The British EIC feared that the influence of Russia over the then current ruler of Afghanistan was too great, so they decided to replace him with their own appointee. In the opening battles, the British captured Kandahar, Ghazni and Kabul.

In 1841 the local Afghans rose up against the British in Kabul and the British garrison eventually had to surrender. They were promised safe conduct to India but were harassed down the Kabul River and were massacred at the Gundamuck Pass before reaching the besieged garrison at Jallahbad. Later the British with a large Indian Army reinvaded and relieved the garrison at Jallahbad.

This website tells this interesting story and provides an excellent introduction to the war and its campaigns.

3.11 The First China War / First Opium War
http://en.wikipedia.org/wiki/First_Opium_War

This was a trade inspired war between the British and the Chinese Qing Empire. It lasted from 1839 until 1842 and it can be said that this war started a long history of Chinese resentment towards Western society.

The Europeans traded heavily with the Chinese and they used their hard currency to buy goods from the Chinese but there was little trade from East to West. The British eventually found that the Chinese had taste for opium so they started selling it to the Chinese. This compensated for the flow of precious metals from the West to the East. However this trade in hard drugs sparked a war. The website gives further details about this interesting period of history.

3.12 Crimean War Research Society
www.crimeanwar.org
The Crimean War Society exists to honour and remember those that fell during this war and to further the study of the war in its entirety. Topics covered include the famous incidents such as the Charge of the Light Brigade, little known aspects of the war such as the British Army's refusal to deploy poison gas at Sevastopol and naval actions in the Pacific.

The Society publishes a quarterly journal called "The War Correspondent". This journal contains recent research studies of the war. The Society also produces a wide array of other publications such as maps, books, information on regimental museum holdings, bibliographies, medal rolls etc.

3.13 Indian Rebellion of 1857
http://en.wikipedia.org/wiki/Indian_Mutiny
This war is also known as the "First War of Independence", the "War of Independence of 1857" by the Indians, or the "Indian Mutiny" / "Sepoy Mutiny" / "Sepoy Rebellion" / "The Great Mutiny" / "The Revolt of 1857" by the British and Western historians. The title "Indian Rebellion of 1857" is currently the modern name for the conflict.

The 1857-1858 war saw armed uprising and rebellions (mainly in northern and central India) against the British occupation of the sub-continent. The war brought about the end of the British EIC's regime and led to almost a whole century of direct rule of the Indian sub-continent by the British.

This website provides an interesting and informative site and has details of all the various battles and campaigns.

3.14 Anglo-Zulu War (at Wikipedia.org)
http://en.wikipedia.org/wiki/Zulu_War
This famous campaign was fought between the British and the Zulu nation. When the war finished it effectively caused the cessation of an independent Zulu nation. It had some bloody battles - the British being decimated at Isandlwana and the famous defence of Rorke's Drift. This site gives one of the best introductions into the

background of this war and how the campaign developed.

3.15 Anglo-Zulu War (at www.genealogyworld.com)

www.genealogyworld.net/azwar/index.html

The Anglo-Zulu war is very well documented here. There is genealogical data such as "Was your ancestor at Rorke's Drift" and "What Happened After". There is a section devoted to the film "Zulu" and it identifies technical issues that are incorrect in the film. The roll call of the defenders of Rorke's Drift is given much coverage but there appears to have been four [different] known versions.

The site elaborates upon the various interpretations and accounts of the battles and comparisons of the numerous accounts are listed on this site. This is an excellent reference site and it is also written in an easy to read format.

3.16 The Second Anglo-Afghan War 1878-80

www.garenewing.co.uk/angloafghanwar/

This website is being developed and it aims to become a major online resource concerning the Second Anglo-Afghan War of 1878-80. It is the home to the "Kabul to Kandahar Database Project" which is a collection of names, family histories and stories concerning those who participated in General Sir F Robert's famous march from Kabul to relieve the besieged garrison at Kandahar in August 1880.

The Database Project intends to list the names of the approximate 9,713 military personnel who undertook this difficult feat and to collect biographical data from descendants in order to provide a living link to this campaign. There are also opportunities for medal collectors to verify entitlement to awards. The research for this project is still being undertaken so it is worthwhile to regularly check the development status of the site.

3.17 The New Zealand Wars

www.newzealandwars.co.nz/index.htm

New Zealand Wars aims to bring together information on the New Zealand Wars of 1845 and 1872. Several generations ago they were known as the "Maori Wars" – being named after the indigenous population. However this term is no longer in favour and seldom used. There have been numerous other names for the wars and they too have drifted both in and out of favour.

The site examines: the causes, the campaigns, the consequences and landscapes. Other sections cover a library, studies and research into these wars. If you are studying these wars this site is informative and well worth a visit.

3.18 Rorke's Drift

www.rorkesdriftvc.com

This famous action at Rorke's Drift on Wednesday 22nd and Thursday 23rd of January 1879 is one of the most famous in all the history of the British military. It was made even more famous with the feature film "Zulu". Some 150 British soldiers defended the supply station at Rorke's Drift against some 4,000 Zulu warriors. This action saw the greatest number of Victoria Crosses (VC) being awarded for one battle in history.

At Rorke's Drift eleven VCs were awarded. The 2nd Battalion 24th Regiment of Foot received seven. One went to each of the Army Medical Department, the Royal Engineers, the Commissariat and Transport Department and the Natal Native Contingent. There may possibly have been more awarded but at the time it was not possible for the award to be issued posthumously.

3.19 The Anglo-Boer War

www.genealogyworld.net/boer/index.html
This site has details of personnel involved and information on how to research ancestors who participated in the war. It has links to other websites covering the war and it lists the "local" units involved in the conflict. There are the muster rolls for local units which detail casualties. This site has useful genealogical data and it is likely to publish more at a later date.

3.20 Anglo Boer War

www.angloboerwar.com
This site has been developed by David Biggins, a member of the OMRS, with the objective of bringing together and making available research, pictures and information about this war. The site was launched in 2004 and it is orientated towards numismatics. It brings together an array of information and has placed emphasis on the biographies of officer casualties and recipients of the VC & DSO. There is data on the main units involved in the war, maps, medal rolls and details of honours & awards.

The main divisions of the website are (1) the main events of the campaign, (2) the main personalities involved, (3) details of Anglo and Boer forces, (4) official and unofficial medals awarded by both the British and the Boers, (5) a breakdown of casualties by unit and an (6) other information section. This website must rank amongst the best on this topic and Mr Biggins has certainly done an excellent job at developing the site.

3.21 Australians in the Boer War

www.pcug.org.au/%7Ecroe/mil_hist.htm
The "Australians in the Boer War" (Oz-Boer War) website is the home for a database covering Australian personnel in the Second Anglo-Boer War. This database makes it easier for genealogists, numismatists, local historians and other researchers to locate and source material dealing with individual Australian personnel. The project has three main objectives:

1)   to provide free online information regarding the soldiers and nurses who served

in Australian (both Colonial and Commonwealth) units that are listed in "Soldiers of the Queen – a Database Index to Boer War Soldiers and Nurses as Listed in Murray" (ISBN 0-947156-16X). This publication was compiled by Dr Robin McLachlan from Charles Sturt University, Brathurst, NSW, Australia. The reference to Murray refers to "Official Records of the Australian Military Contingents to the War in South Africa" compiled and edited by Lt Col P L Murray (RAA – Retd) in 1911.

2) To progressively expand the database to include pointers to other hardcopy sources of information and online resources, and,

3) To ultimately identify and include the thousands of Australians who served in non-Australian units. The emphasis here is to find those who died and were buried but not recognised as Australians.

Thus, this database is an excellent Boer War genealogy reference site.

3.22 The Bedfordshire Regiment in the Boer War
www.rootsweb.com/~engbdf/Military/BedsRegtinBoerWar.html
This site is an extract from the book "The Bedfordshire and Hertfordshire Regiment" by G W H Peters (page 44-55) (ISBN 0-85052-0347). The extract makes interesting reading and brings to life the story of this regiment. It gives the background to the war, the build up and the battles from the perspective of this regiment.

3.23 The Mafikeng Siege – A Cultural Perspective
http://library.thinkquest.org/26852/begin.htm
Before the South African War virtually nobody had heard of Mafikeng. After the siege it became world famous. The siege lasted for seven months and it kept thousands of Boers immobilised. The loss or survival of Mafikeng, located in the outback, was of little real importance to the conduct of the war. This website collates data, has participants' diaries, dispatches from war correspondents and personal reminisces.

3.24 The British Army in the Great War
www.1914-1918.net
This site is very informative about the movements of World War 1 units and formations. The site currently has sections dealing with: Searching for a Soldier, Army Units and Formations, Battles, "Tommies'" Life and Sacred Ground. The Army Units and Formations section is exceptionally useful. The site gives exceptional data on the movements of most British Army battalions and units.

Often, when researching an individual soldier one can identify his Regiment or Unit. This can be done from the medals he was awarded or through research at TNA. Once one knows the name of the appropriate Regiment this website can be used to reveal where and when each unit (battalion) was stationed. The WW1 Medal Rolls at TNA (formerly the PRO) normally identify at least a Regiment, if not a man's battalion, and by using this site an outline of a Tommies' deployments can be made. This site is exceptionally useful for this purpose and is an outstanding resource.

3.25 Iron Harvest

www.ironharvest.co.uk

Iron Harvest has been developing a wide range of products and services that further the understanding of the causes and effects of the Great War. They act as a focal point for battlefield guides and maps, books on the war and battlefield travel.

3.26 Unfortunate Region

www.unfortunate-region.org

This website covers the Great War's battlefields and the individuals involved in the conflict. It has sections on the battlefields, debris found on the battlefields, hardware used in the war, cemeteries and narratives from soldiers / officers.

Its battlefield debris section is really interesting and there are lots of pictures of items found on the Western Front. It is amazing to think that the last time these objects saw daylight was during the horrific events of the Great War.

3.27 World War 1 – Trenches on the Web

www.worldwar1.com

These internet pages contain information on the people, places and events that comprised the ghastly Great War. Entire kingdoms were to vanish in this clash and the map of Europe was re-drawn. This website was created in order to allow readers the opportunity to "explore" the Great War. There is a good reference library and an excellent search facility.

The site is currently maintained by the Great War Society (established in the USA during 1987) (see Section 3.32). It must be noted that there are two Societies which have the same name but different URLs. One is American - the other British.

3.28 The Passchendaele Archives

www.passchendaele.be

The Passchendaele Archives is a project organised by the "Memorial Museum Passchendaele 1917". The battle of Passchendaele in 1917 was one of the greatest conflicts of the First World War. More than a hundred days of fighting resulted in over half a million Allied casualties and the gain of only a few miles of land. The Allied dead mainly comprised of British, Australian, New Zealand and South African troops.

The Passchendaele Archive seeks to create a living memorial to those who fought in the battle. They aim to collate photographs, family documentation and data from military sources. They do not seek to duplicate the excellent database of the Commonwealth War Graves Commission (CWGC – see Section 9.1) and they will only create a "file" if there is a photograph of the man and he died between the 12th

July and 15th November 1917.

3.29 Salonika Campaign Society
www.salonika.freeserve.co.uk
The Salonika Campaign is not as widely known as the Somme, Ypres or Gallipoli but was an important campaign during World War 1. Anglo-French forces landed at the Greek port of Salonika on the 5th October 1915. The purpose of the landing was to provide assistance to the Serbs who had recently been attacked by the combined force of the Germans, the Bulgarians and Austro-Hungarians. However, the intervention came too late to save Serbia and at the end of a bitterly cold winter the Anglo-French troops found themselves back at Salonika. After this defeat the British advised that the troops be withdrawn. The French, with backing from Russia, Italy and Serbia believed that there were still strategic opportunities from remaining in the Balkans so the Campaign continued.

After preparing the port of Salonika for defence, the Allied troops advanced northwards. During 1916 further contingents of Allied troops from Serbia, Italy and Russia arrived and they started an offensive. By November 1916, Monastir had fallen to Franco-Serb forces. During a second offensive in the spring of 1917, the British contingent fought at the First Battle of Doiran (24–25 April 1917 & 8–9 May 1917) but made little impression on the Bulgarian defences. The frontline remained roughly static until a third Allied offensive was mounted in September 1918. The British attacked Doiran for a second time and the Serbs advanced on the Vardar river. The Bulgarians were forced into a general retreat and Bulgaria surrendered on 30th September 1918.

3.30 Western Front Association
www.westernfront.co.uk and www.westernfrontassociation.com
This is the premier organisation for those wishing to research the Western Front of WW1. The WFA has 6,500 members worldwide and produces two excellent journals. They support numerous remembrance and research projects spanning the renovation of battlefield memorials, organising care for veterans and keeping the annual two-minute silence at the Cenotaph in London.

On their website there is the opportunity to take a virtual tour of various famous sites and battlefields such as Ypres, Arras and Loos etc. They have a WW1 trench map service that is restricted to WFA members and their library specialising in WW1 is extensive. They have an active forum where questions and messages regarding the Western Front can be posted. Naturally this facility aids research into this conflict.

3.31 The Great War Society (Est. 1984 in the UK)
www.thegreatwarsociety.com
This Great War Society, established in 1984, is a UK based non-profit making organisation. It is not to be confused with the other Great War Society which was

established in the USA during 1987 (see Section 3.32). The UK society provides a forum for practical research into the uniforms, equipment, weapons, training and daily tasks of WW1 soldiers from both Allied and Central Powers.

Some of the members dress in WW1 costumes, practice WW1 style drill and undertake training and everyday activities as practised by WW1 combatants. The Society is not a battle re-enactment organisation but has a "living history" group.

3.32 The Great War Society (Est. 1987 in the USA)
www.worldwar1.com/tgws
The American Great War Society's website has sections dealing with membership matters, their monthly newsletter, a learning and research centre, and details of the "World War 1 community". It appears that the monthly newsletter is freely available online and that members receive the quarterly journal, "Relevance".

The Society was founded by a group of researchers at the Hoover Institution of War, Peace and Revolution. They subscribed to the belief that WW1 significantly changed the course of 20th century history. The organisation is active, creative and sociable. They have arranged for the flyovers of WW1 aircraft, hosted veteran days, conducted ceremonies at the "Arc de Triomphe", organised film festivals and tours of military installations / museums, and undertaken journeys to France & Flanders.

3.33 The Gallipoli Association
www.gallipoli-association.org
The Gallipoli Association is another not for profit group. They try to preserve the memory of the WW1 campaign in the Gallipoli Peninsula in Turkey which took place between early 1915 and January 1916.

The Association furthers the study of the campaign, and acts as a focal point for those interested in this fascinating campaign. The membership covers authors, specialists, amateur and professional historians and relatives of those who took part in the battles.

Every year, on April 25th, the Association holds a wreath laying ceremony and parade at the Cenotaph (in London, UK) and a service with the ANZACs in Westminster Abbey (also in London). Following these events they have an annual Association Lunch. The Association publishes a quarterly journal ("The Gallipolian"), organises its own tours of the battlefields and offers a bursary award to further the study of the campaign.

3.34 Gallipoli
http://user.glo.be/~snelders/
This site gives details on how to travel to the battlefield and what's there. An excellent history of the campaign is presented on the site and there are interesting light-hearted pages covering things such as "Gallipoli Slang" and "Gallipoli

Weather". It also has comments on the preservation of the battlefields.

3.35 World War 1 Battlefields
www.ww1battlefields.co.uk
This is a little known site which has fascinating pictures of WW1 battlefields. The site is principally divided into sections covering: (1) Flanders, (2) the Somme and (3) other battlefields.

The Flanders section is sub-divided into Essex Farm, Hill 60, Hooge, Langemarck, Messines, Passchendaele, Ploegsteert. Sanctuary Wood, Tyne Cot and Ypres etc. The Somme pages contain graphic images of Newfoundland Park, Thiepval, High Wood, Serre, Fricourt and Mametz. The other battlefields includes Cuinchy, Vermelles, Neuve Chapelle, Ors and Vimy Ridge.

Photographs taken during the battles as well as modern day images are displayed on this interesting website. The images are graphic and bring home the sacrifices made by those who fought during the "War to End Wars".

3.36 FirstWorldWar.com
www.firstworldwar.com
This is an informative website aimed at the general public rather than an academic readership. It covers various topics related to the Great War such as battles at the Somme, Passchendaele and Verdun. There are also articles on poison gas, trench warfare, the famous Christmas truce, machine guns, commanders and light-hearted subjects such as poetry and songs.

3.37 Somme Battlefields
www.somme-battlefields.com
The battlefields of the Somme are a tragic part of modern British history. The First World War shaped the last century and continues to affect our modern lives. After travelling a short distance from the Channel crossing terminals in Northern France one can find the battlefields of WW1. Soldiers in 1914 - 18 made the same journey. However, unlike the modern tourists, large numbers of them did not make the return trip.

The Somme was the site for crucial battles. Critical and intense fighting took place and the soldiers required great endurance, courage and comradeship. These days it is possible to visit these sites whether for a day, weekend or longer. Now, one can walk the front line of 1916 and explore the grounds of historic battles without getting shot.

The site has been developed by the Tourist Board of La Somme and aims to help visitors plan and organise their trips to the Somme. One of the aims of the Tourist Board is to help English speaking visitors gain better access to the region and to help them make the most of their trip.

3.38 Centre for First World War Studies

www.firstworldwar.bham.ac.uk

This is a relatively new site which is administered by the University of Birmingham (in the UK). The Centre for First World War Studies was launched on the 11th November 2002. Its aim is to provide an intellectual and social focus for the University's staff, graduate students and the public who are interested in WW1. The Centre has an outstanding group of "external" members who have contributed to the study of WW1. The Centre aims to be active in developing links with overseas organisations and offers a regular programme of events.

3.39 Salient Points

www.salientpoints.com

This website is designed to be a portal dedicated to the First and Second World Wars. It is a single source of information, references, links, battlefield tourism, books and news. This site provides links to numerous sites dealing with:

- World War 1
- World War 2
- Local history websites
- Organisations and Associations
- Battlefield Tours
- Museums and Attractions
- Re-enactment groups
- D-Day / Normandy 1944, and,
- An associated bookshop

Overall, this is a very useful portal and well worth a visit.

3.40 D-Day

www.normandy-dday.com and www.normandy-tourism.org

On June 6th 1944 the beaches of Normandy in Northern France made their mark in the annuals of military history. It became the battleground of the largest military operation to date. Currently "The Historical Area of the Battle of Normandy" is an open-air museum which brings together all the D-Day sites, museums, places of remembrance and cemeteries.

The website is divided into three main sections (1) latest news, (2) the "Historical Area of the Battle of Normandy" and (3) "Book your D-Day Tour". The second section is very informative and covers the battle, sites, museums and cemeteries.

3.41 Normandie Memoire

www.normandiememoire.com

This site commemorates the D-Day invasion. It is aimed at perpetuating the memory of the battle and acts as a focal point for commemoration. It has informative sections regarding:

- The Atlantic Wall
- Preparations made by the allies ahead of the invasion
- D-Day itself
- The main phases of the Battle of Normandy
- The effects on the local population
- The Navy's role

There is also useful data for researching the battle and these include maps, a chronology of events, a list of civilian casualties, and the "Archives Normandie". For those who may have the desire to visit the conflict sites there is a section on "historical" tourism.

3.42 Juno Beach Centre
www.junobeach.org
The Juno Beach Centre is a museum and cultural centre which opened on 6th June 2003. It is located at Courseulles-sur-Mer, in Normandy (France). The Centre gives details of the Canadian war effort covering both civilian and military aspects. The current Chairman is a veteran and the Centre was established in Canada as a non-profit making organisation. The Minister of [Canadian] Heritage designated the Juno Beach landing site as a site of significant historical site.

One million Canadians served in uniform during WW2 and this site commemorates them. In September 1939 Canada declared war against Germany and this website covers the activities of Canadians in: (a) the Battle of the Atlantic, (b) The Invasion of Sicily, (c) The Italian Campaign, (d) D-Day, (e) The Normandy Campaign, (f) The Battle of Scheldt, (g) The Liberation of the Netherlands and the surrender of Germany.

3.43 D-Day Ancestors
www.ddayancestors.com
This website was launched in 2004 in order to commemorate the 60th anniversary of the D-Day landings. The website's author is a military historian and son of a D-Day veteran. The site lists British soldiers, sailors and air men who were casualties from 6th June 1944 to August 1944. Free data on individuals includes their name, rank, number, date of death, age and the cemetery / memorial where they are interned. Currently the casualty data is listed by regiment and then battalion. Additional data on casualties can be purchased from the website.

There is a list of D-Day cemeteries and these pages give the number of casualties from various nations (e.g. British, South African & Polish etc), historical information on the cemetery and where it is located.

3.44 Combined Operations
www.combinedops.com
During World War 2, Combined Operations played a decisive part in the war effort. Combined Operations undertook many daring and imaginative Commando raids

using the latest technology. The training of hundreds of thousands of personnel in the techniques required for amphibious landings was conducted. This was for D-Day and other major amphibious landings.

This website acts as a focal point for the Combined Operations community. The site is undertaking the development of "Rolls of Honour", a veterans list ("They Also Served"), the creation and maintenance of memorials and the re-enactment of operations.

3.45 Battlefields of World War 2
http://battlefieldsww2.50megs.com
This small site has some excellent nuggets of information on the Battlefields of the last World War. It has details on: (a) the Ardennes, (b) Arnhem, (c) D-Day & Normandy, and (d) the Italian campaign. Using the Italian Battlefields page as an example, the Italian Campaign is sub-divided into Victoria Crosses awarded during the campaign, data on cemeteries, battlefield photographs and a summary of the geography of the various battles constituting the campaign. It is a good site and well worth a visit.

3.46 The Canadian Battlefields Foundation
www.canadianbattleofnormandyfoundation.ca/
The Canadian Battlefields Foundation was founded in 1992. It seeks to educate and actively promote the awareness of Canada's role during World War 2. The site gives a virtual tour of battlefields and the Foundation publishes a newsletter. The activities of the CBF are primarily informative and educational. The CBF offers bursaries to researchers of Canadian Military history. They also:

- organise battlefield tours under the guidance of military historians,
- support group tours to Canadian battlefields in Europe. These trips are organised under the auspices of the Wilfred Laurier University Centre for Military, Strategic and Disarmament Studies,
- run annual trips for Canadian university students
- maintain in perpetuity a garden of remembrance at Le Memorial Museum in Caen (France).
- provide audio-visual and printed historical material.

3.47 Britain's Small Wars 1945-2003
www.britains-smallwars.com
This site covers the history of British military conflicts since 1945. It is dedicated to the men and women who served in these "forgotten" conflicts. The site covers conflicts in India, Palestine, the Malayan Emergency, Korea, the Suez Canal Zone, Kenya, Cyprus, Suez 1956, Borneo, Vietnam, Aden, Radfan, Oman, Dhofar, Northern Ireland, the Falklands, the First Gulf War, Bosnia, Kosovo, Sierra Leone and many more.

Each of the conflicts is covered in detail and some have personal stories as well as campaign histories. There is a section dealing with the campaign medals for post 1945 service, a guest book, details of books covering the campaigns and anecdotes. There are also pages dealing with Special Air Service (SAS) and the Special Boat Service (SBS) which constitute Britain's elite Special Forces.

4   Army Research and History Societies

4.1   *The Arms and Armour Society*
www.armsandarmour.net
This Society was formed in 1950 when a group of enthusiasts decided to form an organisation with the principal aim of studying arms and armour from the earliest time. The Society brings together scholars, collectors, professional experts and others who share a common interest in this subject.

The Society publishes a semi-annual journal which is internationally recognised as the most authoritative in the field and it is the preferred medium for original research papers. A quarterly newsletter keeps members in touch with the numerous events / activities and meetings in the worldwide field of arms and armour.

4.2   *Army Records Society*
www.armyrecordssociety.org.uk
The Army Records Society was founded in 1984. Its objective was, and still is, the publication of documents relating to the military history of Britain. The Society prints an annual journal and membership is open to all (subject to the approval of the Council).

4.3   *Society for Army Historical Research*
www.sahr.co.uk
This Society was formed in 1921 with the aim of fostering interest in the traditions and history of the British Army including the Land Forces of the Empire, Dominions and Colonies of the Commonwealth. The Honourable East India Company which was the forerunner of the Indian Army is also covered by the Society.

The Society's interests covers Army and Regimental history, military pictures and collectables, uniforms and insignia, arms and equipment, traditions / customs and the history of land warfare in general. The study of campaigns, commanders and the politics of war since the 1600s to 1960s are covered. The 1960s cut-off date is due to the lack of primary research material in the public domain and the UK's national archival system.

A quarterly journal is published and this reflects members' interests and their research results. It is internationally renowned for its high standard and its consistently excellent variety, scholarship and content. The Society has also published monographs, bibliographies and soldiers' private papers and diaries.

4.4   *Scottish Military Historical Society*
www.btinternet.com/~james.mckay/dispatch.htm
For more than thirty years the Society has united enthusiasts of Scottish military

history. It has worldwide membership and they enjoy researching the history of Scotland and its associated regiments. The period of study is the 1660's to the present day and the society publishes its findings in their journal entitled "Dispatch". The society studies such issues as the collecting and archiving of primary material, badges and buttons, head-dress and uniforms, plaid brooches, medals, books, picture cards and photographs, prints and watercolours, military equipment and Scottish weapons.

4.5   The Victorian Military Society
www.vms.org.uk
The VMS is an international organisation whose principal aim is to encourage and foster the study of Victorian military history. The period under consideration is 1837 to 1914 which includes the period between Queen Victoria's death and the beginning of the Great War.

The VMS publishes a quarterly journal ("Soldiers of the Queen"), a newsletter ("Soldiers' Small Book") and holds an annual military fair. Additionally, the VMS encompasses the Anglo-Boer War Memorials Project and several other specialist study groups. The specialist groups cover topics such as:

- Anglo-Boer Wars (the first & second)
- India & Burma (the activities of the HEIC etc)
- Sudan Wars (1883-1908)
- 57th Foot (Middlesex Regt) living history group called "The Diehard Company"
- The South Coast Column – a social group covering all topics and periods
- Zulu War – this group encompasses the Anglo-Zulu wars and Zulu history

4.6   The Anglo Zulu War Society
www.anglozuluwar.com
The Anglo-Zulu war of 1879 is one of the extraordinary periods of Victorian military history. The film "Zulu" featuring the heroic defence of Rorke's Drift made this war famous. The first major battle of the war was at Isandlwana. This battle was fought on the same day as Rorke's Drift. The British were slaughtered to the last man at Isandlwana and Rorke's Drift holds the position of being the battle for which the most Victoria Crosses were awarded.

The Society was formed by a small group of experts and historians with the aim of educating, entertaining, enlightening and encouraging the study in the fascinating period of Victorian military history. The Society publishes an online semi-annual journal with accounts of events and theories of the War. The journal also throws light on existing theories by using modern research methods and material.

4.7   The 1879 Group
www.1879group.com
This is another organisation that specialises in the Zulu War of 1879. The Group was founded in May 1998 at the home of the 24th Regiment of Foot (The Barracks at Brecon in Mid-Wales). It has provided a focal point for those interested in this campaign and who share a common interest in the events of 1879 such as Isandlwana and Rorke's Drift.

Most people's interest in this topic started by seeing either or both of the films called "Zulu" (1963) and / or "Zulu Dawn" (1979). These films are very entertaining but there are a number of incorrect technicalities (see also Section 3.15). The truth was that the men had stained helmets, faded tunics and were battle hardened veterans. They did not wear crisp scarlet tunics with bright white pith helmets.

4.8   The Australian Light Horse Association
www.lighthorse.org.au
The Association is a non-profit organisation whose aim is the preservation of the history and tradition of the Australian Light Horse and its predecessors. The site is dedicated to the Light Horse Regiments and the Light Horsemen who served their country. There is information on both historical and current affairs, data on famous regiments, details of battles and primary information from the viewpoint of the ordinary horseman.

4.9   The Indian Military Historical Society
http://members.ozemail.com.au/~clday/imhs.htm
This small society was formed over a decade ago. It acts as a forum for the dissemination of knowledge regarding: medals, uniforms, buttons, badges, other militaria from Indian units, and the history of the formations which existed before and after Independence.

Units of the Royal Navy, the British Army and Royal Air Force formations that served in India, plus units of the HEIC's marine and land forces are considered as suitable research subjects. Also, Indian Army and Navy units after 1861 including the European Volunteer Corps, The Royal Indian Marine, Royal Indian Navy, the Army of Nepal and those of the Princely States and post-Independence units of the present day India, Pakistan, Bangladesh including Frontier Corps, Para Military and Police units come under the Society's remit.

The Society publishes an interesting quarterly journal called "Durbar" and covers research into the above mentioned organisations and their history.

4.10 The South African Military History Society
www.rapidttp.co.za/milhist/
The South African Military History Society was formed a few decades ago with the

purpose of studying and promoting the study of military history. It currently has around 500 members who are principally located in the major cities of Johannesburg, Durban & Cape Town.

The activities of the Society are: (1) the semi-annual publication of the "Military History Journal", (2) monthly lectures in South Africa, (3) monthly newsletters, (4) both day and weekend visits to battlefields.

4.11 The New Zealand Military Historical Society
http://homepages.ihug.co.nz/~phil/nzmhs/
This organisation was formed to foster the study of New Zealand (NZ) military history, wars that have occurred within NZ and New Zealanders at war. It also seeks to encourage research into, and the study of, NZ military traditions, uniforms and insignia and weapons. The NZMHS publishes a journal three times a year called "The Volunteers" and they hold an informative monthly lecture.

4.12 The Scots at War Trust
www.fettes.com/scotsatwar/aboutsaw.htm
The Scots at War is a charity which promotes:

- research into Scottish military affairs,
- the collation of material, and,
- to make available to the public information on Scots at War

The trustees do not seek to collect artefacts, medals, papers etc but will advise as to where they may be suitably deposited. The Trust has a commemorative roll of honour, an information service, access to specialists and expert facilities. It also runs a lecture / seminar series.

5   Associations for Ex-Service Personnel

5.1   *Army Benevolent Society*
www.armybenfund.org
The Army Benevolent Fund is the Army's national charity. Since the end of World War 2 the fund has helped soldiers, former soldiers and their families in their time of real need. The charity provides timely advice and financial support to four generations of Army families, the physically disabled, the mentally ill, the unemployed, the homeless and the elderly.

The ABF works in partnership with Regimental and Corps Benevolent Funds, and other Service charities to identify, investigate and provide (financial) support to individuals. Financial support is given to individuals via Regimental / Corps Benevolent Funds. Usually an ABF grant supplements whatever the Regimental / Corps have been able to provide.

Additionally, help is provided through large grants from the ABF to other charitable organisations which provide for the special needs of a soldier or an ex-soldier and / or their family.

5.2   *Association of Jewish Ex-Servicemen*
www.ajex.org.uk
The Jewish Ex-Servicemans' Legion was formed in 1928 and became the Association of Jewish Ex-Servicemen and Women in 1939. AJEX had its beginnings in meetings held in London in 1928. At one of a series of meetings, held in Britain, to protest at Arab anti-Jewish riots in Palestine more than a thousand Jewish ex-servicemen crowded into the Grand Palais Theatre located in the east end of London. Many more were unable to gain entry to this meeting and an important resolution was passed that day which called for a formation of a Jewish Ex-service organisation. The response was immediate and the Ex-Service Legion was formed. Nowadays, AJEX serves the needs of ex-service personnel and continues to act as a focal point for them.

5.3   *The Last Post Association*
www.lastpost.be
Every evening since 1928, at precisely 20:00 hours the Last Post has been played at the Menin Gate Memorial to honour those fallen in World War 1. The Last Post is the traditional salute to the fallen warrior.

This daily tribute which is performed by a team of local buglers honours the memory of the soldiers of the British Empire who gallantly fought and died in vast numbers at the Ypres Salient during the Great War.

The aim of the Society is to perpetuate this moving and emotional ceremony.

Visiting the Menin Gate Memorial is in itself very moving but hearing the Last Post being played there is even more emotional.

5.4   The Royal British Legion
www.britishlegion.org.uk

The Royal British Legion is the UK's leading charity providing support - financial, social and emotional - to the millions who have served, current service personnel and their dependents. At present about 11 million individuals are eligible for support and the Legion receives around 300,000 calls for help every year.

Founded in 1921 as a voice for ex-service personnel, it continues this work with nearly 550,000 current members. Although the needs of ex-service personnel have changed over the years, the Legion is still there to provide support, safeguard their interests and welfare and perpetuate their memory. British service personnel are in action world wide and they know that if they need the Legion's support – now or in the future – the Legion will be there on active duty.

5.5   The Royal Canadian Legion
www.legion.ca

There are many veterans' organisations in Canada but The Royal Canadian Legion is the largest with over 400,000 members and affiliates. In addition, there are about 58,000 members of the Ladies Auxiliary who provide invaluable support to the Branches of the Legion.

The Legion is a not-for-profit organisation which is supported through membership dues and membership is open to current and ex-service personnel of the Canadian Forces, Royal Canadian Mounted Police (RCMP), The Royal Newfoundland Constabulary, other Police forces and their dependents. Since it was formed in 1925/6 the Legion has focussed efforts to ensure adequate pensions and other benefits for veterans and their dependents. It also acts as a lobbyist to the Canadian Government on the affairs of ex-service men and women.

The Legion strives to maintain the perpetuity of the annual Remembrance Day. Funds raised through the sale of poppies goes to help veterans and ex-service personnel who are in need.

5.6   Veterans Agency
www.veteransagency.mod.uk

The Veterans Agency is part of the UK's Ministry of Defence and it deals with military pensions and compensation. Pensions have been paid to ex-service personnel since the reign of Queen Elizabeth 1st. Naval pensions were funded from the "Chatham Chest" which raised funds from a charge of 6d a month from the wages of every officer and rating. Later the "Chatham Chest" was transferred to the Royal Greenwich Hospital and the Army's pensions came under the Royal Hospital at Chelsea.

The huge number of casualties and wounded in the 1914-18 war proved that the old arrangements were insufficient to meet the demands for pensions and compensation. The War Pension Scheme was created and it dealt with the pensions for all three services. In 1917 the Ministry of Pensions was created and it later became the Department of Social Security.

World War 2 saw the scope of the Ministry of Pensions widen to include ex-members of the Polish Forces who served under British command, Merchant Seamen and civilians injured due to enemy action. Since WW2 there have been many other conflicts and any disablement due to these conflicts or any other service can lead to the award of a War Pension.

5.7   The Machine Gun Corps Old Comrades Association
www.machineguncorps.co.uk
The trenches of the Great War gave rise to the tactical development of these lethal weapons. During these bloody battles the machine gun was the queen of the battlefield. In each and every major battle – Somme, Ypres, Vimy, Arras and Verdun etc – the machine gun decimated whole battalions. The machine gun changed warfare strategies and inflicted huge casualties.

The "Machine Gun Corps Old Comrades' Association" was formed after WW1 by its veterans. It still survives today but the membership profile has changed from veterans to the descendents of veterans and those interested in the Machine Gun Corps. There are only six known members who served in WW1 and they have all attained the glorious age of at least 100 years old.

Unfortunately, the official documents of the MGC have been ill-fated. Most were lost during the Blitz (in World War 2) but the papers of individual companies and battalions that did survive are now held at the Imperial War Museum (see Section 8.2). Numerous personal diaries & papers have also been donated to the IWM. War Diaries for companies and battalions are at the TNA and are available for public inspection.

5.8   The Burma Star Association
www.burmastar.org.uk
The Burma Star and the Pacific Star with Burma Clasp are the two (British) awards for service during the Far Eastern campaign in World War 2. Those personnel whose service entitled them to both stars only received the one they qualified for first and a clasp (bar) for the second award was issued. It is relatively common to find the Pacific Star with Burma Clasp.

The qualification for either star was one or more days of operational service during the Burma Campaign which took place between 11th December 1941 and the 2nd September 1945. Membership to the Association is open to those who qualified for either one of the awards. Their website lists obituaries, individual servicemen's stories, tales about battles, a diary of events and a discussion forum.

The Association's aim is to relieve need, hardship or distress among the men and women who served in the British or Allied Forces or in the Nursing Services during the Burma Campaign of the Second World War. Help is also extended to their service personnel's widows, widowers or dependents.

5.9   Far Eastern Prisoners of War Association
www.fepow-community.org.uk and www.fepow.org.uk
This Association was formed in 1947 shortly after the prisoners were released from Japanese POW camps. The Association's motto is "To keep going the spirit that kept us going". There are a number of branches to the Association, each one being autonomous but amalgamated under the umbrella of the "National Federation of Far Eastern Prisoner of War Clubs and Associations (NFFCA).

5.10   Taiwan Prisoners of War Memorial Society
www.powtaiwan.org
This site covers the story of the Japanese prisoner of war camps on the island now called Taiwan (it was formerly known as Formosa). It describes the stories of the men who were interned there. The Society is committed to locating where the camps were and writing their history. They want to honour and commemorate the men who never made it back home.

5.11   Japanese Prisoner of War
www.west-point.org/family/japanese-pow/
These pages are dedicated to the memory of the POWs who died whilst in Japanese hands during WW2 and to those that survived this horrific era. The purpose of Japanese-POW is to assist the descendants who want to know more about their relatives' experiences. It is an informative site and a useful research guide.

5.12   The National Ex-Prisoner of War Association
www.prisonerofwar.freeservers.com
This Association promotes the welfare of those POWs from the UK or allied forces and to renew the spirit of comradeship. The Association keeps lists of Allied POWs in German & Italian hands during WW2. There is no definitive list for POWs in Japanese hands during WW2 and the records for WW1 are very patchy. Details of all known POWs and those reported as missing in action during the Korean War are available.

5.13   British Armed Forces and National Service
http://britisharmedforces.org
This site deals with both Regular and National Service personnel. It covers all three branches of the armed services, has testimonials from ex-servicemen and histories of various formations. The National Service Act was introduced in 1939 at the

outbreak of WW2. The site covers the history of the (conscripted) military from this date until National Service ended in 1963.

The majority of National Servicemen went into the Army and they made up half of the force. National Servicemen were in action alongside their Regular comrades in Korea (1950-53) and at Suez. The last intake of National Servicemen was in 1960 and the last National Serviceman was demobbed in May 1963. This website deals with issues surrounding these conscripts in an interesting and informative manner.

5.14 Forces Reunited
www.forcesreunited.org.uk
Forces Reunited is the leading UK Armed Forces Reunion website. It holds the largest UK database of current and former members of the British Armed Forces. Forces Reunited lets individuals find their old friends and former colleagues.

5.15 Comrades and Colleagues
www.comradesandcolleagues.com
This site enables you to search for comrades and colleagues from principally the British and Commonwealth Armed Forces. Their database holds details of thousands of military units from all around the world, including the British Army, Royal Navy, Royal Fleet Auxiliary, Australian Army, Royal Australian Navy, Royal Australian Air Force, New Zealand Army, Royal New Zealand Navy, Royal New Zealand Air Force, Canadian Army, Navy & Air Force etc.

5.16 Soldiers', Sailors', Airmen and Families Association (SSAFA)
www.ssafa.org.uk
SSAFA is a national charity helping ex-Service men / women and their families including widows / widowers. It can trace its roots back to the "Soldiers' and Sailors' Help Society" which was formed in 1885. The eligibility criteria for help from the SSAFA is one day's paid service in any of HM Forces or National Service. For those who served in the Reserves a period of satisfactory service is necessary to qualify for aid.

5.17 Royal New Zealand Returned and Services' Association
www.rsa.org.nz
The Royal New Zealand Returned and Services' Association is a NZ service organisation. It is one of the largest voluntary welfare organisations in NZ and one of the longest established veterans associations. Today it has about 130,000 members who are spread throughout NZ and they share a common commitment to the Crown, the Nation and the Community.

The RSA's commitment to the welfare of ex-service personnel is embodied in the annual Poppy Day. The poppies are exchanged for donations. These funds are then used to help the ex-service men / women and to perpetuate the memory of those who have been killed whilst in service.

5.18 Women's Royal Army Corps Association

www.wracassociation.co.uk

During the First World War (in 1917) women were recruited for the first time to serve with the Army in a non-nursing capacity. This gave birth to the Women's Army Auxiliary Corps (WAAC). The WAAC later changed its name to Queen Mary's Army Auxiliary Corps when Queen Mary became its patron. The QMAAC was disbanded in 1921 and the Army Territorial Service (ATS) was created in 1938. The ATS was the female part of the British Army during WW2. More than a quarter of a million women served in the ATS and the contribution the ATS made was widely recognised. Plans were made for a peacetime female force and in 1949 the Women's Royal Army Corps was instituted.

The WRAC Association was formed at the same time as the WRAC in 1949. The Association superseded the Army Territorial Service (ATS) Old Comrades Association and the aims of the Association are to:

- foster the esprit-de-corps and the well being of the ATS / WRAC
- keep former members of the ATS / WRAC in touch with each other and keep alive their comradeship
- to act as a link between former and current members of the ATS / WRAC
- help current / former members who are experiencing hardship via the ATS & WRAC Benevolent Fund

5.19 The First Aid Nursing Yeomanry (Princess Royal's Volunteer Corps)

www.fany.org.uk

Formed in 1907, the Corps was "to be of assistance to the military and civil authorities in time of emergency". Their purpose is still the same today as it was when they were established. The FANY was formed to be a first aid link between the frontline fighting units and the field hospitals. During WW1, FANYs ran field hospitals, drove ambulances, organised soup kitchens and canteens for the troops. This work was often done under very dangerous conditions and by the end of WW1 the FANYs had been awarded 17 Military Medals, 1 Legion d'Honneur and 27 Croix de Guerre (the latter two being French decorations).

FANY formed the nucleus of the ATS Motor Driver Companies during the Second World War. One section was attached to the Polish Army and a Kenyan unit was formed in 1935. Some FANYs joined the Special Operations Executive (SOE) and went on dangerous missions in occupied Europe. FANYs saw action in all theatres of war including North Africa, Italy, India and the Far East.

Since WW2, the Corps has been known chiefly for its work in the field of military & civil communications and it was officially renamed in 1999 as the "Princess Royals' Volunteer Corps (PRVC)" – it is now commonly called FANY (PRVC).

5.20 Armed Services Assistance Centre Inc (Australian)
www.asacaustralia.com
The ASAC Australia provides free assistance to serving and ex-serving members of the Australian Defence Forces They give advice on pensions, welfare, compensation and entitlements. This site also includes information on the wearing and award of military medals to Australian personnel (see Section 6.10).

5.21 Vietnam Veterans Association of Australia
www.vvaa.org.au
The Vietnam Veterans Association website was formed to provide information of special or current interest to Australian Vietnam Veterans. Secondly, it aims to provide to the public historical information about Australia's involvement in this war. The latter covers data on units / formations and personnel issues.

The VVAA has campaigned for many years regarding the use of chemicals during the Vietnam War and their effects on Australian service personnel. They also try to help to alleviate hardship amongst their membership.

6 Medals and Awards

6.1 Orders and Medals Research Society

www.omrs.org.uk

The Orders, Decorations and Medals Research Society of Great Britain was established in 1942 by a group of four individuals who had been meeting informally since 1939. Their intention was provide lengths of medal ribbons and to exchange information about ribbons. Over time the group grew and they started publishing the "Circular". At the time, the "Circular" was one of the few publications that dealt with numismatic subjects.

By 1958 the "Circular" had become the "Journal" and membership was growing in leaps and bounds. During 1958 the name of the Society was changed to "The Orders and Medals Research Society". Currently, the OMRS has branches worldwide and has helped to promote the wealth of material published regarding medals and awards.

The OMRS holds an annual banquet and convention which usually takes place in September. As well as the main journal, the specialist branches of the OMRS provide two magazines namely the "Broadsheet" for the Miniature Medals Branch and "Ribbon Collector" for the Ribbons Branch. The OMRS's publications are amongst the most informative that are available on this topic.

6.2 The Victoria Cross Website

www.victoriacross.org.uk

Often the recipient of this most prestigious honour did not live to tell their tale. As well as giving an index to VC holders, this website gives details of the last resting place for VC holders. It is possible to get the location of VC holders' graves sorted by counties and countries. There are also details of the burials overseas in places like Ireland, France and Belgium etc.

The known locations of VCs are listed and it is possible to conduct a search based upon the recipient's name. Data on those VCs in Regimental museums and those held by other organisations are given. Usually details of a recipient's full set of medals are given on the website and there are details of recent VC sales.

6.3 The Victoria Cross

www.victoriacross.net

This informative site contains data on the awarding of this great honour. The awards can be searched by the recipient's name, unit, rank, location of the brave deed, campaign, nationality. Further details are given of living recipients and VCs on public display.

6.4   Victoria Cross Heroes

www.victoriacrossheroes.com

The Victoria Cross (VC) is Britain's most prestigious military honour, awarded for valour in the presence of the enemy. From the Crimea to Iraq, it has been bestowed only 1,355 times. This indicates just how restricted it is to the exceptional bravery required to gain its award.

Lord Ashcroft began collecting Victoria Crosses in 1986 at Sotheby's in London. Since then he has established a trust to look after a collection that has grown to more than 140 VCs. The collection contains about one tenth of all the VCs awarded to date. They cover all three services and spans from the Crimean War (1854) to the Falklands War of 1982. At the time of writing the Collection is due to go on public display in London

6.5   George Cross Database

www.gc-database.co.uk

The George Cross was instituted in September 1940 to recognise civilian gallantry at the height of the Blitz. King George VI created this award for Commonwealth citizens, both male and female, whose heroism could not be rewarded by any other honour. The site gives details of recipients.

6.6   Orders, Decorations and Medals

www.medal.net

This website serves as a portal from which various links can be followed. The topics covered include medals, research services, associations, auction houses, militaria dealers, defence issues and government departments.

6.7   Medals Awarded to New Zealand Military Personnel

www.nzdf.mil.nz/medals/index.html

This website features the more common medals which have been awarded to New Zealand (NZ) military personnel since the NZ Wars of the 1840s and 1860s. It does not cover the medals issued to personnel in small numbers or in unique circumstances. NZ military history is strongly interwoven with British military history and New Zealanders were eligible for a vast array of British awards.

In the last two decades the awards and honours systems of both the UK and NZ has been overhauled. Now indigenous NZ awards have now replaced British military and state awards. The main focus of this site is on military awards. However military personnel can and do receive State awards which are also issued to civilians. Hence, both British and NZ State Honours are reviewed on this site.

6.8   New Zealand Honours

www.dpmc.govt.nz/honours/overview/index.html

The history of the NZ honours system mirrors changes in the country's constitution.

It started as a Crown Colony, changed to a Dominion and from a Dominion into a fully independent monarchy or realm. From 1848 to 1975 NZ shared the British based honours and awards system. Between 1975 and 1996 the NZ honours system was a mixture of the British and NZ honours. Then on the 6th May 1996, NZ's honours system became fully independent.

The NZ Royal Honours System, administered by the Honours Secretariat, is comprised of:

- The Order of New Zealand
- The New Zealand Order of Merit
- The Queen's Service Order and Medal

There is also a series of Gallantry and Bravery Awards. Gallantry Awards include:

- The Victoria Cross for NZ (VC)
- The NZ Gallantry Star (NZGS)
- The NZ Gallantry Decoration (NZGD)
- The NZ Gallantry Medal (NZGM)

And bravery awards are:

- The NZ Cross (NZC)
- The NZ Bravery Star (NZBS)
- The NZ Bravery Decoration (NZBD)
- The NZ Bravery Medal (NZBM)

The website gives further information on the criteria etc of these awards.

6.9 Veterans' Affairs Canada - Canada Remembers
www.vac-acc.gc.ca/remembers/
Once arriving at this site, it is best to use the sitemap to find the "Canadian Orders, Medals and Decorations" page. Canada now issues medals of its own. The principal categories for Canada are: (1) Orders and Decorations, (2) Modern Honours (post 1972), (3) War Medals (1866–1918), (4) War Medals (1939–1991), (5) United Nations medals, (6) International Commission Medals, (7) War Service Badges, (8) Memorial Crosses, (9) Commemorative Medals and (10) Efficiency / Long Service Decorations and medals. These awards reflect the changing nature of Canada as it has progressed from a British colony to an independent state.

6.10 Australian Medals
www.asacaustralia.com/medals.htm
This is an interesting site regarding the award of medals to Australian personnel. There are details of:

- Service and Campaign medals pre-WW1
- Service and Campaign medals for WW1
- Service and Campaign medals WW2
- Service and Campaign medals post WW2

They also handle medal applications and give details as to the rules and regulations for wearing medals.

6.11 Medals of the World
www.medals.org.uk
This site is informative and useful for identifying unknown medals. It essentially consists of medals and images of medals from all over the world. It is catalogued on the basis of the country / state issuing the award. A country profile can contain: (a) a ribbon chart, (b) a list of orders, decorations and medals for that country and (c) links and other references to the medals of the target country.

6.12 The Indian Order of Merit
http://faculty.winthrop.edu/haynese/india/medals/IOM/IOM.html
The origins of this award date from the times of the HEIC. The original proposal was for a decoration that would reward military achievement and for which both Indian officers and men would be eligible. The General Order establishing the decoration stated that it was to "afford personal reward for personal bravery, without reference to any claims founded on mere length of service and general good conduct". This website is an invaluable tool when researching this award which eventually blossomed into the "Order of British India".

7 Archive Facilities

7.1 The National Archives

www.nationalarchives.gov.uk

The National Archives (TNA) was formerly called the Public Record Office (PRO) and it is the main archive facility in the UK for British Government records. The military archives at the TNA essentially cover three main areas:

- Records relating to individuals
- Records relating to campaigns, battles or actions
- Records relating to units, battalions and formations

For a military researcher the TNA's archives enable him to search:

- Personnel records for individuals who left the military before approximately 1920,
- Medal rolls to confirm entitlement to medals,
- War diaries and other documents relating to formations' active service. These documents may cover the affairs of a particular company or battalion,
- Data on the history etc of various units.

The TNA's archives are vast and it is impossible to give a full account here. Not only are the British Government's records available for public inspection but the TNA has an extensive library.

The TNA's material principally covers British and related forces / formations who were under British command. The TNA publishes numerous research leaflets and books regarding their holdings. They provide an excellent overview of the available material and how to conduct various searches. These leaflets are an invaluable guide when conducting research at the TNA and their usefulness cannot be under-estimated. The TNA also has an extensive bookshop which is accessible over the internet and this shop has many of the TNA's specialist publications.

It should be noted that records for the Indian Army are kept at the Oriental and India Office located within the British Library.

7.2 The British Library

www.bl.uk

The British Library (BL) is one of the main archival facilities in the United Kingdom. The Library holds a copy of every publication which has been published in the UK and its holdings are therefore vast. For military history, the main departments within the British Library are (1) the Newspaper Collection and (2) the Asia, Pacific and African Collections (APAC). The APAC section of the BL includes what is commonly referred to as the Oriental and India Office Collection

(OIOC) or the "India Office Records". The holdings of both of these departments are huge so only a brief summary is below.

7.2.1 National Newspaper Collection

www.bl.uk/collections/newspapers.html

The Newspaper Collection holds numerous publications covering newspapers and magazines. The following notes are aimed at aiding research into British Military history between 1801 and 1945.

Newspapers contain a wealth of information and may include:

- biographical details of soldiers, sailors and air men,
- information on a unit, battalion, ship, regiment etc
- accounts of specific battles or campaigns taking place in any theatres of conflict.

Regional newspapers are often excellent sources of facts and data on individuals, regiments and battalions. During the Boer War and both World Wars local newspapers often published:

- weekly casualties and / or obituaries
- memoriam notices

- gallantry awards obtained by local men
- data on local regiments / battalions
- graphic details of events at the front

There are a number of newspapers held in the collection that are of interest to the military historian. Some of the lesser known ones are:

- The Police Gazette – This paper includes a weekly list of 'Deserters and Absentees from His Majesty's Service' covering all three branches of the Armed Forces. This publication is closed for 75 years and people wishing to see Police Gazettes less than 75 years old need to obtain written permission from the Metropolitan Police, New Scotland Yard.
- War Office Weekly Casualty List – This list was started in WW1 with the aim of providing accurate and comprehensive data on those killed, wounded, missing and captured in all theatres of conflict.
- The Territorial Service Gazette – Established in 1859 this publication is useful for research into the army's territorial battalions especially during WW1.
- Lloyd's List – This publication contains many reports & accounts about the war at sea. It contains casualty lists and obituaries of merchant navy and fishing fleets personnel. Also details of decorations to RFC / RAF & RNAS for attacking enemy shipping and U-boats were included.
- The Aeroplane – Material included in this journal covered a weekly "Roll of Honour" (listing RFC / RAF & RNAS personnel), obituaries of the fallen and information relating to promotions & bravery decorations. There was also information on those confirmed as being 'in the hands of the enemy'.

7.2.2 Oriental and India Office Collection in the Asia, Pacific and African Collections (APAC)

www.bl.uk/collections/asiapacificafrica.html

As stated earlier the Asia, Pacific and African Collections (APAC) department at the BL includes the Oriental and India Office Collection (OIOC). The reading rooms at the BL's King's Cross site still refer to the section as the OIOC or the abbreviation "The India Office". The correct title is the "India Office Records in the Asia, Pacific and African Collections".

The India Office Records are the documentary archives of the administration in London of the pre-1947 Government of India. They comprise the archives of the East India Company (EIC) (1600–1858), the Board of Control / Board of Commissioners for the Affairs of India (1784–1858), the India Office (1858–1947), the Burma Office (1937–1948) and a number of related British agencies overseas.

The main series of documents in the India Office dealing with military affairs is the "L/MIL" series. These documents are the military records for the India Office and cover the whole spectrum of military affairs of both the EIC's armies and the armies of the Government of India. They cover military policy, defence schemes and the organisation of the army, navy (marine) and air force in India.

The careers of individual officers and soldiers in the Indian Army, the Indian Medical Service and the Royal Indian Navy (including the Bombay Marine and the Indian Navy) can be researched. Medal rolls, prize and batta[2] rolls and soldiers' letters are included in this document class. There are also records of soldiers' and cadets' entry into military service in England prior to embarkation.

At the India Office there are details of military pension scheme arrangements. They cover the Poplar Pension Fund (for the officers & seamen of the EIC marine), the Lord Clive Military Fund (for European officers & other ranks of the EIC / Indian Army), the Bengal Military Fund (for the widows of officers, surgeons and chaplains of the Bengal Army), the Bengal Military Orphan Society (for the children of officers, chaplains and surgeons of the Bengal Army), the Madras Military Pension Fund (for the widows / children of officers, chaplains and surgeons of the

---

[2] BATTA ROLLS – These are rolls of officers and / or soldiers who are entitled to "Batta" payments. Sometimes public servants were also eligible. Payments were generally made for service in the field or on special grounds. Batta payments can be considered as a sort of "prize money" which was awarded to troops after a battle. The word Batta is believed to originate from Hindi. The reference for this is "Hobson-Jobson – A Glossary of Colloquial Anglo-Indian Words and Phrases, and of Kindred Terms, Etymological, Historical, Geographical and Discursive" by Col. Henry Yule and A C Burnell, 2nd Edition printed by Routledge & Kegan Paul, in London, Boston, Henley, Kitab and Madras.

Madras Army) and the Indian Military Service Family Pension Fund which provided benefits to the widows and children of officers, surgeons and chaplains of the Indian Army.

Although the majority of military related papers are held in the L/MIL series there are associated documents kept by the India Office's War Staff organisation (the "L/WS" series). They maintained their own files on military strategy, organisation, intelligence and supply. Their papers are available at the IO and it is advisable to use the book "Guide to the Records of the India Office Military Department" by A J Farrington (London 1982) as a guide when searching the IO's collection.

7.3   Access to Archives (A2A)
www.a2a.org.uk
No note on military based archive facilities would be complete without mentioning this excellent website. The A2A database contains catalogues describing the archives held on a local and national level in England and Wales. The entries in the catalogues range from the eighth century to the present day. At the time of writing the A2A site stresses that their catalogue does not yet offer a full description of all local archive facilities but it is regularly updated.

This site is not just a military based archive but it does hold considerable data pertaining to the armed forces. It is an excellent catalogue for both the British and Indian (HEIC and the Indian military up to Independence). When starting a research project it is often a good idea to try this site to see if there are any appropriate hits.

The A2A database contains over 10 million records relating to 9.2 million items held in 408 record offices and other repositories. The archives are cared for in local record offices and libraries, universities, museums, national institutions and specialist organisations across England and Wales.

Even if individuals, families or groups are not mentioned in the catalogue they may be mentioned in the primary source material. It is important to check the catalogue for hits as they could well be documents which contain data on the individual, group or family.

7.4   Scottish Record Offices and Archives on the Web
www.oz.net/%7Emarkhow/scotsros.htm
This is a useful site if you are researching Scottish affairs. It primarily acts as a site which has links to Scottish Record Offices and Archival bodies. This site is exceptionally useful when one is trying to find Record Offices. Some military records such as those for the Army's Territorial Forces are held locally and organised at the County / District level.

7.5 Public Records Office of Northern Ireland
www.proni.gov.uk
This archive facility is included for completeness but sadly its holdings are relatively limited. It does have data from some large collections. Papers from the Castle Stewart, Castlereagh, Graham, Armstrong of Lisgoole, Nugent of Farren Connell, Hart, Kilmorey, Leslie, Schomberg MacDonnell, Staples, Templehouse, Treasury Solicitor and Wynne collections are all held.

In addition the PRONI has data on Militia, Yeomanry and Muster Rolls. These documents are arranged by county and include pay lists, lists of officers and musters.

7.6 Library and Archives of Canada
www.collectionscanada.ca/war-military/index-e.html
This website is the official site for the Library and Archives of Canada. Some of its collection is in digital format and it has virtual exhibitions which you can visit. The digital collections include information on Canadian soldiers in the Boer and the First World War. Other topics such as the Canadian War Industry in WW2 are also covered.

The South African War (2nd Boer War) of 1899–1902 is a key event in Canadian military history. It was the first occasion for which Canadian troops were sent to an overseas theatre of war. A total of 7,368 troops and 12 nursing sisters served in South Africa. The data on this website brings together the three groups of records pertaining to this conflict namely, the personnel records, medal registers and land grant applications.

Over 600,000 Canadians were enlisted in the Canadian Expeditionary Force (CEF) during the Great War. The CEF database is an index to the personnel files which are held by the (Canadian) National Archives. To date, over 800,000 images of Attestation Papers (service records) have been scanned and are available online.

Of interest is the digital database for WW1 Canadian Expeditionary Force (CEF) Unit War Diaries. From the start of the war all CEF units had to maintain a daily account of their actions. These were called "Actions in the Field" and they are more commonly referred to a Unit War Diaries. They are not personal diaries but rather a historical record of a unit's administration, operations and activities during the First World War. They can be obtained via this website.

7.7 The International Committee of the Red Cross
The International Site is at *www.icrc.org* and the British Site is at *www.redcross.org.uk.*
The International Committee of the Red Cross, based in Geneva, keeps list of all known Prisoners of War (POWs) and internees of all nationalities for the Second

World War. Enquiries about POWs / internees should be sent to:

> Archives Division and Research Service, International Committee of the Red Cross, 19 Avenue de la Paix, Geneva CH – 1202, Switzerland

7.8   Liddell Hart Centre for Military Archives
www.kcl.ac.uk/lhcma/top.htm
This is part of King's College London University and it holds the private papers of over 500 senior British defence personnel who held office during this and the last century (1900–2005). Their archives contain information on WW1, WW2, the Korean War and the Berlin Crisis. They also hold data on American defence issues such as its relationship with the USSR, Cuban Missile Crisis etc. but these are out of the scope for this book.

Particular classes of information that are relevant to the British Army researcher are D-Day (1944), the Arnhem offensive, Dardanelles (1915), Argentine records for South Georgia (Falklands War 1980s) and the Daily Mirror collection (1914-1916).

Other potentially useful classes are: French Resistance Operations in Normandy during 1944, WW2 maps relating to Greece & Burma, Pamphlets relating to the British War Effort (1940-45), Press cuttings relating to the Boer Wars, the First Balkan War, Irish Home Rule and the British Army in Ulster (1881-1921), publications relating to the British Army in North Africa and Italy during World War Two, Records of the Joint Chiefs of Staff (1942-53), British Intelligence ULTRA messages (1941-45) and WW1 Trench maps. The Archive also has data on the history of Nuclear weapons.

7.9   New Zealand Military Personnel Records
www.nzdf.mil.nz/personnel-records and www.archives.govt.nz
This section of the NZ Defence Force's website provides information on the awarding of medals and details of those able to examine the Service Records of ex-Service personnel. They handle all queries relating to the award and entitlement of medals. Those medals not issued during the lifetime of the recipient can be awarded to the next of kin.

The NZ Defence Force Personnel Archives holds the personnel files of individual servicemen who were discharged from 1899 (the Anglo-Boer War) to the present day. The archive covers the Navy, Army and Air Force. They do not hold any other military archive materials. The Personnel Archives (at Trentham Military Camp) holds some 1.5 million personnel files relating to 420,000 NZ service personnel. These records are an invaluable and unique historical resource.

It should be noted that the Chief of the Defence Force and the Chief Archivist of Archives New Zealand have agreed to transfer all files of personnel who served in the NZ forces up to and including 31st December 1920 into the permanent care of Archives New Zealand.

Approximately 6,000 personnel records for the South African War have been transferred to the Archives NZ. The records of the 92 South African War veterans who served after 1920 are still at the NZDF Personnel Archives. About 170,000 files for the First World War are currently being transferred to the Archives NZ and the transfer process will take until at least 2006.

7.10 Australian Military Personnel Records

www.naa.gov.au/the_collection/family_history/armed_services.html
The National Archives of Australia's holds a collection of records regarding service in the Australian armed forces. They date from the creation of the Federation in 1901. The military records can be divided into:

1. *World War 1 (1914 - 1918).* These records regard those who served in the Australian military (i.e. the First Australian Imperial Force / Australian Flying Corps / Australian Naval and Military Expeditionary Force / Royal Australian Naval Bridging Train / Australian Army Nursing Service). Data on Home / Depot units for personnel who served within Australia is also available.

2. *Second World War (1939 – 1945).* The Archives hold the service records of Australians who served in WW2. Copies of these can be purchased from the Archives or viewed on the site. The Australian Army personnel record for a WW2 soldier typically consists of:

   - the Attestation Paper (covers next of kin, age, trade & other personal details),
   - Service and Casualty forms (B103) which record information about units and postings, injuries and disciplinary charges
   - a Discharge form that summarises the person's service
   - a head and shoulders photograph of the soldier
   - other documents and / or correspondence

3. *Service after World War 2.* The size and contents of personnel files for the Australian Army (and the Royal Australian Air Force) vary considerably so it is difficult to specify a file's contents.

7.11 Churchill Archive Centre

www.chu.cam.ac.uk/archives/
The Churchill Archive Centre at Churchill College, Cambridge University, is the home to the papers of Sir Winston Churchill and to more than 570 collections of personal papers and archives documenting the history of the Churchill era and after.

7.12 National Archives of Scotland

www.nas.gov.uk
The holdings of the NAS are vast and we will only consider military records here.

Accounts for the Army during 1639–1659 have been published and the NAS holds very few records relating to individuals serving in the Scottish Army before 1707. It is possible to find Officers' Commissions in the warrant books from 1670 and in private papers.

For post-1707 research there are:

- Exchequer Records – relates to the settlement of soldiers on forfeited estates after the Jacobite Rebellion
- Private Papers – various records are kept here and they vary from orders of battle to personal correspondence
- Wills – the final testaments for Scottish soldiers

Militia, lieutenancy and yeomanry units' papers dating from around 1800 are stored at the NAS.

7.13 National Archives and Records Service of South Africa
www.national.archives.gov.za
The holdings of the National Archives and Records (NASA) exceed 140 kilometres of shelving space, comprising of records in a variety of media. These records reflect the activities of governments in South Africa since the middle of the 17th century. The records are generated at national, provincial and local government level and cover various issues.

The facility does hold some military genealogical data and it is worthy of note that they hold the records for the South African Constabulary (SAC). The SAC consisted of numerous British men who served in this unit during the South African War of 1899-1902.

7.14 The Liddle Collection
www.leeds.ac.uk/library/spcoll/liddle/index.htm
The Liddle Collection was founded in the 1970s with the aim of collecting and preserving first hand individual experiences of the Great War. The archive includes original letters and diaries, personal and official papers, newspapers and artwork, photographs and written and recorded recollections.

The material in the Collection includes the personal papers of over 4,000 men and women from WW1 and of about 500 people who experienced WW2. The papers are grouped by geographical area in which the person served and by the nature of their military service.

7.15 Hillsdale College
www.hillsdale.edu/personal/stewart/war/
Hillsdale College was established in the USA during 1853. The College has a collection of primary source material relating to military affairs. The collection is

currently focused primarily on European military history prior to the 1900s. There is the intention to incorporate American, non-Western and contemporary military history and it is believed that these topics will be incorporated at a later date.

The online holdings encompass 405 documents, 2 maps and 1 secondary source. Gradually all the documents are being placed into PDF format. The "Documents in Military History" section has subsections on:

- Ancient and Medieval history
- The English Civil War
- Colonial Wars
- The American Revolution
- The Napoleonic Period – the War of 1812

- Mexican – American Wars
- The Crimean War
- The American Civil War
- The Franco Prussian War
- The Spanish American War, and,
- The First World War

7.16 BBC WW2 Peoples' War
www.bbc.co.uk/ww2

The BBC has developed a site to record individuals' personal experiences of the Second World War. The site is dedicated to capturing people's personal stories of WW2 whether military or civilian. It is an internet only project and all contributions have to be made over this media.

A large portion of the content on this site has been sourced from reminisces of those who experienced the war at first hand. The site is commonly referred to as "The WW2 People's War" and it stopped accepting contributions from the public at the end of January 2006. The site has now been frozen and archived.

The site enabled viewers to join discussions, add stories and photographs, question researchers and to be a volunteer helper. The site has information on how to research family history and has articles on various topics such as medals and the insignia worn on uniforms.

The site has specialist "desks" where users can put research questions to discussion lists which others with a similar interest contribute and subscribe to. The research desks cover general military affairs, the merchant navy, the Home Front and there is one for each branch of the forces.

8   National Museums

In this section we consider the larger museums which are generally national in nature. There are numerous smaller museums dealing with the history of a regiment, corps or other formations. In the UK, there are approximately 150 museums dedicated to regimental histories. For the sake of brevity these Regimental museums are not reviewed individually. However, Appendix F gives a list of Regimental Museums and the regiments, units, formations and corps in which they specialise. Appendix F also gives the known web address for the Museums.

It should be noted that the Army is trying to collate a listing of Regimental Museums and they are developing their website, *www.army.mod.uk/museums/index.htm*, as a result. A lot of regiments do have their own site. At present, the official Army site currently points to the Army Museums Ogilby Trust when one searches for particular museums.

8.1   The National Army Museum
www.national-army-museum.ac.uk
The National Army Museum is the British Army's own museum. It is the only museum which tells the story of the British land forces from the battle of Agincourt in the 1500s to modern day peace-keeping missions (in the twenty first century), and the history of Commonwealth land forces up to their respective dates of independence.

The Museum is an excellent place for information on the general history of the Army but it holds few official records. It does have an excellent library which is one of the best regarding the British Army. The main repository for official government records is however "The National Archives" (see Section 7.1).

8.2   The Imperial War Museum
www.iwm.org.uk
The IWM was founded to commemorate WW1 and it is the major British museum for wars since 1900. The collections have expanded over time and they encompass a wide range of articles including works of art, documents, films and photographs, sound clips, books and maps. All branches of the military are covered and some civilian fields as well.

The Department of Documents holds a vast number of diaries, letters and personal papers covering topics like wartime service, prisoners of war and internees (in Europe & the Far East), conscientious objection, refugees from Nazi persecution and civilian life. There are also papers from various high-ranking officers, records on the military and economic history of the Axis powers during WW2 and documents on the War Crimes Trials.

The Museum's collections include 6,500 hours of videotape and around 120 million feet of film. The Film and Video Archive at the museum is the official repository for such films and they are considered to be public records. There are approximately 6 million still photographs and this collection is also a national repository. For researchers, this is an excellent opportunity to access photographs and films from various twentieth century conflicts.

8.3 The Army Museums Ogilby Trust
www.armymuseums.org.uk
The Army Museums Ogilby Trust serves the regimental and corps museums of the British Army. It supports the development of the museums displaying the regimental / corps collections of the British Army. The regimental and corps museums in the UK display and contain a wealth of information on the units of the British Army and sometimes individuals who served in such units.

On this website there is the extremely useful feature which allows you to search for a regimental / corps museum. This is exceedingly useful when trying to discover a formation's history or to initiate contact with the Regimental museum. You can run a search based on a either a Museum or a Region. Unfortunately, not all museums are named according to the Regiment(s) they are based upon. One example of this is the Keep Military Museum which contains the collections of the Regiments of Devon and Dorset including Militia and Volunteer Units. Who would have guessed the name of the Museum for this regiment?

On the website there is a list of the Historical Regimental Names and this gives some indication of lineage and titles for units. Appendix E is based upon this list and it indicates all known Regimental Museum websites. Again, the name of the museum may not always be obvious so one has to examine the list.

8.4 The Anglo Boer War Museum
www.anglo-boer.co.za
One of the main events in the history of South Africa is the Anglo Boer War of 1899 to 1902. Although the protagonists were the British and the two Boer Republics the whole population of South Africa became involved either directly or indirectly. The War Museum at Bloemfontein gives the visitor an insight into this conflict and via its art collection, dioramas and exhibits it brings the war "alive". The course and development of the War unfold in front of the visitor and glimpses of what life was like in concentration camps and POW camps are given. This museum is a must do for those serious students of the history of South Africa and the Boer War.

8.5 National War Museum of Scotland
www.nms.ac.uk/war/home/index.asp
Countless numbers of Scots have been involved or touched by wars and military service. The military has left its mark on Scotland and it is possible to explore this history in the magnificent setting of Edinburgh Castle.

The museum houses uniforms, insignia, equipment, decorations, medals, weapons, silverware and paintings etc all of which have a story to tell. At the Museum you can see fascinating documents and photographs from both official and private sources. These items uncover hidden stories of courage and heroics.

8.6   South African National Museum of Military History
www.militarymuseum.co.za
The South African National Museum of Military History, situated in Johannesburg in the Province of Gauteng, is the only museum of its kind in South Africa. It provides a nucleus of military history expertise in southern Africa.

South Africa did not establish a national museum to recognise the role its troops had played during WW1 but this failure was addressed when South Africa entered the Second World War. Captain J Agar-Hamilton was appointed the official historian of the Union Defence Forces and he formed a Historical Research Committee in order to preserve documents and material of military interest. The Museum is the South African equivalent to the UK's Imperial War Museum which was established to acknowledge the sacrifices made by Britain.

9   Graves, War Memorials and Rolls of Honour

The following sites deal with graves, Rolls of Honour and memorials to the war dead. Most of the sites deal with the dead from post-1914 conflicts. The recording of details for the war dead before 1914 was not conducted with the same efficiency as those after 1914.

Often pre-1914 war graves may be marked by something as simple as a few stones with no headstone or nothing at all to indicate a burial. Burials were likely to occur on the battlefield and often in haste with the location ill-recorded. The resting place of Victorian soldiers is seldom identifiable today but there may be a memorial tablet to commemorate the fallen.

It is recommended that those seeking details of British war graves dating before 1914 write to: Ministry of Defence, PS4 (CAS) (A), Room 1012, Empress State Building, Lillie Road, London, SW6 1TR

9.1   Commonwealth War Graves Commission
www.cwgc.org
This is an excellent website for researching post-1914 British and Commonwealth casualties. It is the official site for the Commonwealth War Graves Commission (CWGC). They manage and attend to the cemeteries and memorials to those killed since 1914. They have a database containing the details of casualties including data such as unit, place and date of death, home address, next-of-kin, age and decorations. This database is usually referred to as the "Debt of Honour Register". Records can be searched by name or battalion / unit. This helps tracing casualties from a unit during a particular battle or campaign. There are also some civilian casualties on the CWGC website.

9.2   UK National Inventory of War Memorials
See *www.iwm.org.uk*
The UK National Inventory of War Memorials is accessible through the Imperial War Museum's website. Currently this project is in the information gathering phase and a database of War Memorials in the UK is being developed. It is estimated that there are between 50,000 to 60,000 memorials.

The memorials exist in different forms, from the frequently seen crosses or plaques to buildings, gardens of remembrance, lynch gates, hospitals, chapels and windows. The inventory lists the unique place these memorials have in our history. The inventory covers not only the World Wars but also the many other conflicts that the British Army has been involved with.

9.3   The British War Memorial Project
www.britishwargraves.org.uk
This is a voluntary project to build an online International War Memorial to British Service Personnel from 1914 to the present day. It includes those killed in recent conflicts as well as those in peacekeeping operations. The contributors to this site have visited over 3,000 cemeteries and have over 90,000 records and photographs.

You can search the site based upon a name or service number, unit, branch of service, cemetery, county and country. It is possible to obtain pictures of the specific grave or commemoration.

9.4   Lost Generation
www.channel4.com/lostgeneration and
www.channel4.com/history/microsites/L/lostgeneration/index.html
This site was launched in late 2005. Ninety years ago a whole generation was almost annihilated on the muddy trenches of the Western Front and the other gruesome battlefields of WW1. Their dreams, aspirations, hopes and lives were ripped from them and this website now offers the public the opportunity to turn those long lists of the war dead back into real people.

The site offers the ability to search for names on memorials to the fallen and to search for memorials recording various details. There are informative sections on family history, the Home Front, the Somme and a database of WW1 weapons.

9.5   UK Roll of Honour
www.roll-of-honour.com
This is a site dedicated to those who fell fighting for the UK. The site is organised by county and there are entries for Scotland, Wales, Northern Ireland, the Channel Islands and the Isle of Man.

The war memorials and rolls of honour cover a variety of regiments, units and airfields. Memorials overseas are also included.

9.6   Soldiers Died in the Great War 1914 – 1919
www.great-war-casualties.com
This site is the home for the sale of the CD-ROM of the same name which has details of over 703,000 soldiers killed in World War 1. The CD-ROM was first issued in 1998 and the second edition is now on sale. The CD-ROM is fully searchable and an invaluable tool for research.

The origins of this site are based on the series of volumes of casualties created after WW1. Eighty one volumes of information on the casualties of the Great War were published in 1921. These volumes listed every regiment and corps of the British Army and contained about 635,000 soldiers and around 37,000 officers who died in

WW1. 'Soldiers Died' contains the complete 81 volumes and the CD-ROM is searchable via regiments, battalions, surnames, Christian name(s), initial(s), place of birth (town and county), where enlisted (town and county), regimental number, place where they were killed in action, whether died of wounds, theatre of war, date of death.

9.7   Irish War Memorials

www.irishwarmemorials.ie

This website presents an inventory of war memorials in Ireland. The main purpose of the site is to make available information on Irish casualties to genealogical researchers. It includes photographs of and the inscriptions on each memorial. The features of each memorial are also noted. There is a database of those mentioned on the memorials and it is possible to search for individual names. For each name there is a link to photographs of the appropriate memorial.

Many of those mentioned on the memorials are included in lists in books dedicated to the fallen. These books are generally derived from lists of casualties and published rolls of honour. If applicable, information on the book in which an individual is listed is given on the website.

9.8   War Memorials Trust

www.warmemorials.org

The War Memorials Trust is the only UK charity working solely to conserve and protect the estimated 65,000 war memorials in the UK. The Trust originated in the mid-1990s in response to rising concern regarding the neglect of and the occasional vandalism of memorials. The Trust widened its remit in 1999 by developing a maritime branch to protect naval (military) vessels that had sunk with loss of life. The Trust can supply information on a wide range of issues regarding war memorials such as grants and funding (for memorials), guidance and advice on projects and to offer individuals the opportunity to become involved in the protection of memorials.

9.9   Australian War Memorial

www.awm.gov.au

During the Gallipoli campaign (1915) of World War 1 C E W Bean (the Australian Official War Historian for the First World War) first began thinking of developing a site to commemorate the sacrifice of the Australians. The idea of a national museum took place later whilst Bean was visiting Pozieres, in France, where more than 23,000 Australians were casualties in less than seven weeks fighting in 1916. Bean's idea was to create a place in Australia where families and friends could grieve for those buried or missing many miles from home. Even today the commemoration and furthering the understanding of war inspires the work at the Memorial.

During WW1 Australian troops were officially encouraged to collect relics and some of those are now on display in the Memorial. Documents, artefacts and media are actively collected by the Memorial. The Memorial holds one of the best document and media collections in the world.

The Memorial holds extensive data. There are databases that can be searched for either research or family history purposes. Personal service records, Rolls of Honour, Commemorative Rolls, various Nominal Rolls and a database of honours and awards are at the Memorial. There are digitised images of approximately 32,000 individuals' case files for Australian personnel reported as wounded or missing during World War 1. Details of the 23,000 Australian Military Forces (AMF) personnel who were either prisoners of war or recorded as missing during WW2 operations in the Far East / South West Pacific Islands are also held at the memorial.

9.10 War Memorials in Australia
www.skp.com.au/memorials/
This site lists locations, descriptions and images of war memorials in the states and territories of Australia. Memorials include monuments, honour rolls, buildings, and a variety of utilitarian facilities. They were all erected in honour and remembrance of those who served their country during wartime and gave their lives.

The site is in two parts: (1) an index and (2) detailed descriptions. The index has basic data such as location, type, number of names and what the memorial commemorates. If possible a photograph is included. As for (2) the detailed description includes all of the data in (1) plus names and inscriptions. The descriptions take more time to complete so they lag behind the entries in (1). In August 2005, the site had indexed 5895 memorials and had detailed descriptions of 963 memorials.

9.11 Leaders of ANZACs – Officers of the Australian and New Zealand Army Corps Who Died at Gallipoli 1915
www.anzacs.org
These pages list the 'Officers of the Australian and New Zealand Army Corps Who Died at Gallipoli in 1915'. Recorded on the site are the names of 492 ANZAC officers who are known or believed to have died as a result of their service on the Gallipoli Peninsula, Turkey, in 1915.

9.12 Canadian Virtual War Memorial
www.vac-acc.gc.ca
The Canadian Virtual War Memorial website contains a registry of the graves and memorials of more than 116,000 Canadians and Newfoundlanders who served valiantly and gave their lives for their country since Confederation. There are details of casualties from all the major conflicts as well as the smaller, less-known conflicts. Included are details of more than 100 Canadians who have been killed in service since the Korean War and the fallen from Peacekeeping Operations and other operations.

The memorial is trying to collect photographs of the individuals who have died so a digital image of them can be held for posterity. The main purpose of the memorial is to recognise and keep alive the memory of the achievements and sacrifices made by those who have served the nation. It is possible to search the memorial for individuals based upon their name.

9.13 "We Will Remember" – Canadian War Monuments

www.cdli.ca/monuments/index.htm

Canadian War Monuments are indicative of the price many Canadians have paid to preserve the Canadian way of life. This project is an attempt to preserve the hundreds of war monuments across Canada. Digital photographs have been taken of the monuments in order to make the data available to a wider audience via the Internet. It is possible to search for War Monuments in Canada. This is done via a menu where you can select the appropriate State and the search returns a list of monuments in the specified state.

9.14 National War Memorial, New Zealand

www.unknownwarrior.govt.nz and www.nationalwarmemorial.govt.nz

New Zealand's National War Memorial consists of the War Memorial Carillon and the Hall of Memories. It commemorates the New Zealanders who lost their lives in the South African War, World War 1 and 2, Korea, Malaysia and Vietnam. An unknown NZ warrior is interred in a specially constructed tomb at the National War Memorial.

9.15 South African War Graves

www.southafricawargraves.org

The goal of the South African War Graves Project is to photograph every single South African and Rhodesian war grave. The wars covered include the Second Anglo-Boer War, World Wars 1 & 2, Korea, more recent conflicts such as the Rand Revolt, the Freedom Struggle, the Angola-Border War and others right-up to the present date. The photographs are either in the form of a headstone or a name on a memorial. The photographs will be freely available to certain groups of people like next of kin.

Due to the distances and cost involved many families and friends of the fallen, from South Africa and Rhodesia, cannot visit the graves in person. By developing an archive of these memorials, this website is able to fill a chapter in many people's lives by sending to them photos of the last resting place of a loved one.

9.16 South African Graves for Australians in the Boer War 1899 – 1902

www.hagsoc.org.au/sagraves/nmcdb/nmcdb-search.php

The Heraldry and Genealogy Society of Canberra (in Australia) has developed this searchable database of Australian soldiers who were killed in the Boer War of 1899–1902. The Australian Department of Veterans' Affairs helped with the funding and the National Memorial Council of South Africa provided the records of Australians from their Victims of Conflict database.

9.17 World War 1 Cemeteries
www.ww1cemeteries.com
This website is organised around a book published in 1929 called "The Silent Cities". This book by Sidney C Hurst gives details of all the 940 cemeteries with over 40 burials. All of these sites have been visited personally by the website's owner and numerous photographs have been taken.

The site contains details of other military cemeteries and memorials from all around the world and there are details of:

- Cemeteries in Belgium
- Cemeteries in France
- Cemeteries with Victoria Cross burials
- Cemeteries of those "Shot at Dawn". Those men who were executed under the Army Act during the Great War

9.18 Military-Genealogy.com
www.military-genealogy.com
This is a website developed by the Naval & Military Press. It is a commercial site and gives details about the fallen in both World Wars. When Great Britain went to war in 1914 its army numbered just over 247,000 men. It also had an additional 486,000 Reservists and Territorials. By November 1918, almost a further five million had enlisted.

Not only does this site have links to data on WW1 army casualties, it also houses the WW2 "Army Roll of Honour". This Roll contains the details of WW2 British Army casualties. The WW2 Roll of Honour was previously maintained by TNA in document class WO 304. That list has now been computerised and placed into a searchable database. The Army Roll of Honour can now be used and utilised by researchers, genealogists and military historians.

To access the details of the casualties in either war you need to subscribe to the site and depending upon the data required there are various cost structures.

9.19 Silent Cities – A Guide to the Cemeteries and Memorials of the First World War in France and Belgium
www.silentcities.co.uk
This site contains an alphabetical index to all the First World War cemeteries and memorials in France and Belgium. Those cemeteries in which a Victoria Cross holder is buried are noted and so too are those with military executions (i.e. those executed under British Military Law). The last resting places for soldier poets are also recorded.

9.20 British Officers Died (1750 to Present Day)

http://members.tripod.com/~Glosters/memindex3.htm

This site aims to be a memorial to those officers listed as killed in the line of duty. The index covers numerous wars, battles and campaigns and the lists have been compiled from various books, casualty lists, newspapers, medal rolls and memorials. The conflicts covered are: North America (1750–1782), Peninsular Campaign, Napoleonic Battles, Afghanistan (1838–1842), Sutej Campaign (1845-1846), Punjab Campaign (1848–1849), Crimean War (1854–1856), Indian Mutiny (1857–1859), Afghanistan (1878–1880), South Africa (1879), Egypt (1882) and Sudan (1896–1897), Boer War (1889-1902), North West Frontier in India (1895-1902), Rhodesia (1896), India (1908), Irish Rebellion (1916), Malaya (1948-1960), Korea (1950–1953), Northern Ireland (1969–1999), Falklands (1982), Kosovo (1999) and Afghanistan and Iraq (2003–2004).

There is special coverage of the Gloucestershire regiment's officers who were killed during the World Wars.

9.21 Soldiers Memorials

www.angelfire.com/mp/memorials/memindz1.htm

This is a sister site to that in Section 9.20. Whereas the other site considers officers died, this site covers NCOs and other ranks. It has an alphabetical section for graves in India. Other sections cover, for example, The Indian Mutiny (1857-8), Umbelya (1863), Malays (1875), Perak (1876-77), Kabul Residency (1879), the Boer War, Singapore Mutiny (1915) and memorials in Burma.

There are sections for certain elements of the RAF & RN, and there are regimental memorials covering the Artillery regiments, certain Dragoons & Lancer regiments. In addition, there are "Assorted Memorials" covering specific units, formations and regiments. The final section covers known Rolls of Honour.

9.22 Australian Service Nurses National Memorial

http://members.optushome.com.au/lenorefrost/nurses.html

Australian nurses who died during or as a result of war service since the Boer War are commemorated here. The 'Australian Service Nurses National Memorial' is dedicated to their memory and the National Memorial is located in Canberra, Australia.

The Returned and Services Nurses Club of Victoria (Australia) is preparing a list of all Australian Service nurses who have served overseas since the Boer War up to the First Gulf War (1991). It is believed that this second list of those who served will be co-located at this site.

9.23 Australian War Graves Photographic Archive

www.australianwargraves.org

The Australian War Graves Photographic Archive used to be called the AIF

(Australian Imperial Forces) Remembrance Project. It is committed to creating a digital archive of every Australian war grave and commemorative memorial for Australian personnel. The not-for-profit project is a tribute to the 112,000 Australians who never made the return journey alive and whose remains are scattered worldwide across cemeteries in 83 countries.

As the project progresses, memorials and graves from the Boer War, WW1 & 2, Korea, the Malaya Emergency, the confrontations with Indonesia, Vietnam, the Gulf Wars and casualties from Peacekeeping Operations will be recorded and catalogued.

9.24 Australian World War 2 Nominal Roll
www.ww2roll.gov.au
The (Australian) World War Two Nominal Roll was created to honour and commemorate the men and women who served in Australia's Defence Forces and the Australian Merchant Navy. The site contains information from the service records of some one million service personnel who served during WW2. It is possible to search the site by name or service number, honours, place (of birth, enlistment or residential locality at the time of enlistment) and to print a certificate of service for individual soldiers.

9.25 British Association for Cemeteries in South Asia (BACSA)
www.bacsa.org.uk and *www.bl.uk/catalogues/indiaofficeselect*
It is estimated that the mortal remains of some two million British and other Europeans – soldiers, civilians and their families – lie throughout the Indian sub-continent.

BACSA was established in 1977 in order to protect these cemeteries. Since then BACSA has done much towards their restoration and maintenance. In addition they have sought to record inscriptions. The geographical region covered includes India, Pakistan, Bangladesh, Sri Lanka, Burma, Malaysia, Singapore, Indonesia and Thailand. Surprisingly, they also consider some parts of the Arab world albeit the title of the organisation includes the words "South Asia". There is no statutory body or government agency with the responsibility of caring for these cemeteries and therefore without the support of individuals, via BACSA, many of these cemeteries would quickly disappear.

BACSA members have meticulously recorded and photographed inscriptions on numerous gravestones and monuments and this wealth of information is housed within the British Library's Oriental and India Office (see Section 7.2.2). From its database, BACSA has published over forty books on cemetery records, with details of names, inscriptions and biographical notes on individual tombs / gravestones. BACSA has set-up an on-going project to record the monumental inscriptions in the UK which relate to British connection with South Asia.

The society's journal is called the "Chowkidar" and is circulated to members every six months. This journal contains reminiscences of members, reports on members'

63

visits to South Asia and it acts as a forum for discussing the condition / whereabouts of specific graves. The organisation publishes memoirs and biographies and these publications give a fresh insight into the social, military, business and administrative life of Europeans in the East.

10 Publishers, Newspapers and Magazines

10.1 Naval and Military Press
www.naval-military-press.com
This site is ideal for military book enthusiast. It is possibly the largest website dedicated to military books. The Naval & Military Press was formed in 1991 and has over 25,000 worldwide customers enjoying their publications.

10.2 The Armourer
www.armourer.co.uk
This magazine is published by "Beaumont Publishing Ltd" which was established in 1994. It covers everything from militaria, arms, armour, weapons and is ideal for enthusiasts and collectors. Usually there are featured articles on ordnance, medals, bayonets, insignia and uniforms, military museums and battlefields etc.

10.3 Medal News
www.tokenpublishing.com
Token Publishing was formed in 1983 to publish one magazine called "Coin and Medal News" – this was a magazine that had been in circulation in one form or another since 1964. The title was split into two during 1989 and formed respectively "Coin News" and "Medal News". Medal News is probably the best "monthly" journal in circulation in the UK regarding military medals. Published ten times a year the magazine features articles, news, auction reports and the well known medal tracker service. The medal tracker service is invaluable when searching for lost medals and those trying to re-unite broken groups

They also publish an excellent book called "Medal Yearbook". This is an essential reference publication regarding British and Commonwealth medals. In the current version there are details on Canadian, Australian, New Zealand and South African awards.

10.4 Military Modelling Magazine
www.militarymodelling.com
This magazine serves the military modelling community. It is a specialised journal and features articles on figures, vehicles, dioramas and miscellaneous topics. Examples of content include articles on military modelling societies and shows, the modelling work undertaken by readers / associates, and technical details appropriate to the modeller.

10.5 War Time News - Veterans' Magazine
http://wartimenews.co.uk
This title was launched in 1995. Since then it has grown and it now has worldwide readership. Each issue contains personal reminiscences of WW2, many of which are

being published for the first time, and details of events that made the news over sixty years ago.

Written by veterans "Wartime News" features their personal experiences of war. Today, those memories are still as strong as ever. People from all walks of life contribute to this title and they don't just feature the main battles and events. They try to get unique and interesting stories written by ordinary men and women. Stories from WAAFs, POWs, Bomb Disposal, air crew, merchant navy and those who served on the home front – like the Land Army, Civil Defence and Home Guard. Readers recall the good times, rekindle the camaraderie spirit, and share memories and experiences.

10.6 Battlefields Review
www.battlefields-review.com
"Battlefields Review" is a magazine that has contributions from leading military historians and experts that allow the reader to appreciate battles and battlefields. Regular features cover news, a diary of events and interviews with key figures in military history. The interesting website supplements the printed version of the magazine.

10.7 Soldier Magazine
www.soldiermagazine.co.uk
This magazine is aimed at the serving soldier and it has articles on various topics of interest to the professional soldier. Features include army training, veterans' affairs, details about respected and known personnel, reviews of kit and equipment, historical issues (e.g. the battle of the Somme), and current operations of British and foreign troops.

10.8 The War Times Journal
www.wtj.com
The War Times Journal (WTJ) is an on-line magazine that covers all periods of military history and science. The WTJ's goal is to present good quality articles and archives relating to wars and armed conflicts. There is an emphasis on publishing eye-witness accounts and personal experiences.

They also offer free war-gaming rules, a store where you can buy gaming miniatures and books. There is no charge for accessing the content of the website and the owners rely on the patronage of the shop by the readers. Its business model works as the WTJ has been on-line since 1996.

10.9 Pen and Sword Books
www.pen-and-sword.co.uk
This company publishes books on most areas of Military History. Their site is updated weekly and contains many special offers and features. Their catalogue is divided into thirteen main areas. They are: (1) Napoleonic, (2) pre-WW1, (3) WW1,

(4) WW2, (5) post-WW2, (6) Falklands, (7) military biography, (8) military reference, (9) regimental histories, (10) battlegrounds, (11) local histories, (12) military classics and (13) Pen and Sword Select.

10.10 Derek Hayles Military Books

www.dhmb.co.uk and www.militarybooks.co.uk

This commercial site specialises in carefully selected books dealing with the campaigns, wars, personalities and logistics of the British Army from the earliest times to the present day. The directory for the site has categories for pre-1914, WW1 / WW2, militaria, biographies and it has a very useful unit history section. The bookshop is UK based and all prices are in Pounds Sterling (GBP £). As a service to clients they operate a "wants list" for those elusive books that are difficult to obtain.

10.11 Tom Morgan Military Books

www.fylde.demon.co.uk/welcome.htm

This site used to belong to "Ray Westlake Military Books" however it has been taken over by Tom Morgan. It specialises in books on the First World War and offers an interesting selection of books for sale. There is a link from the home page to the catalogue of books. The home page has sections covering Great War News and Information, guides to the battlefields, war memorials, details of certain individuals who served during 1914-18 and general interest articles.

11 Battlefield Tours

11.1 Waterloo Battle Tours Ltd

http://waterloobattletours.users.btopenworld.com/

This company specialises in guided tours to the battlefield of Waterloo. Their tours are usually limited to a group size of 6 to 10 people per tour and they offer an attractive package. During the tour they visit Le Caillou, Quatre Bras (where the Brunswick Monument is), the main battlefield, Lion Mound, La Haye Saint and Hougoumont Farm.

11.2 Flanders Tours

www.flanderstours.co.uk

Flanders Tours' product portfolio covers the entire length of the Western Front of World War 1. They have been visiting the battlefields for over two decades and during that time they have encountered numerous French and German devotees. They endeavour to give the tourist a wider perspective of these historic events and they pay tributes to soldiers on both sides of the conflict. Often a focal point for a customer is the pilgrimage to the cemetery or memorial where a relative is commemorated or a particular area of action. Flanders Tours offer such personal visits at no additional charge.

11.3 Somme Battlefields Tours Ltd

www.battlefield-tours.com

Somme Battlefields specialise in self-drive and conducted tours to the Somme and Ypres battlefields of the Great War. It is run by a husband & wife and they have been operating for almost a decade. They don't employ tour guides but accompany all of their conducted tours. Their tours are particularly suited to the discerning battlefield visitor who may select to visit the battlefield in a small and friendly group.

11.4 Battlefield Tours

www.battlefieldtours.co.uk

This website also offers tours of battlefields. It is not to be confused with a company offering similar products and having a similar name (see Section 11.3). This site is organised by "The War Research Society / Battlefield Tours" and has been operating for a number of years. During that time it has taken thousands on visits of the battlefields, memorials, and to see the last resting place of the fallen. They offer guided historical tours of the areas of both of the First and Second World Wars in Northern France, Belgium and Italy.

Their WW2 product portfolio includes trips to France, Belgium, Holland, Germany, Poland, Italy, Singapore and Thailand. Furthermore they have expanded their range and it is also possible to visit battlefields located in South Africa (e.g. Zulu & Boer

Wars).

11.5 Midas Tours
www.midastours.co.uk
Midas Tours was formed in 1993 and since then they have arranged numerous
escorted tours of worldwide battlefields. They operate tours to the Western Front,
North and South Africa, and Russia. Their broad portfolio covers WW1 & 2,
Napoleonic, 19th Century (Zulu, Boer, India, and the Crimea), and ancient and
medieval battlefields. They have escorted units from the British Army as well as the
general public to various battlefields. The army has considered their tours to be of
educational benefit and often patronise this company.

11.6 Holts Tours
www.holts.co.uk
Holts Tours has (in 2004) been incorporated into the Titan Group of Companies.
Their tours span ancient and medieval campaigns, battles related to revolutions &
empire building, and a staple diet of tours to battlefields of World War 1 and 2. They
have a broad range of tours for each of the categories they serve and they have an
extensive list of experts who escort the tours.

11.7 Leger Holidays
www.leger.co.uk
Leger Holidays is a "general" tour company and undertakes many tours that are not
related to military topics. They do have a section dealing with Battlefields and the
following comments refer to that division of the company.

Leger's battlefield tours cover Belgium, France, Holland, Luxembourg, Italy, Poland
and Germany. Both World Wars are considered and there are trips to famous sites
like the Battle of the Bulge, Arnhem (Operation Market Garden), Colditz, the D-Day
beaches, Ypres, Flanders and other Western Front sites.

11.8 Tours with Experts
www.tours-with-experts.com
"Tours with Experts" offer escorted visits to historical sites of conflict throughout
the world. They have tours for the English Civil War, the Napoleonic Wars, the
American Civil War and the two World Wars.

12 Re-enactment Groups

12.1 English Civil War Society

www.english-civil-war-society.org
The main aim of this society is to stimulate interest in the authentic reconstruction of army life during the seventeenth century and by doing so, to entertain and instruct both the society's members and the public.

The society has two elements – the King's Army and the Roundheads. They gather at "musters" held throughout the campaigning season which lasts from March to October and they re-enact events of this turbulent period in English history. The Society has been active for 25 years and it has conducted considerable research into the war.

12.2 Napoleonic Association

www.n-a.co.uk
The Napoleonic Association was formed for those people with a common interest in the period of history starting with the French Revolution through to the battle of Waterloo. Whether researching the battles of Napoleon and Wellington or recreating battles of the period, the Association has a lot to offer.

The best known activity of the Association is their re-enactments. These activities deal with recreating the life of soldiers and camp followers. Some 30 units (commanded by Allied, British, French, North American and Australians) make up the army's infantry, artillery and cavalry. The Association holds regular small events and 2 to 3 times a year they have major gatherings.

The Associations research department has sections that deal with:

a) The British Militia and Volunteers
b) The Honourable East India Company
c) The French Commanders
d) Russian Army
e) German States
f) Engineering, Surveying and Cartography
g) The Women and Non-combatants

12.3 The Sealed Knot

www.sealedknot.org
The Sealed Knot is an English Civil War Re-enactment organisation. Every year they help to bring history alive at period houses throughout the UK. The Sealed Knot has been heavily involved in education for many years and they have given displays and talks about the Civil War to many schools.

The principal aims of the group are to promote research into, the study of and the development of public interest in the history of the English Civil War. They do this by:

a) The performance of re-enactments of battles, sieges and other events.
b) The organisation of lectures, discussion forums, the publishing of books and the recording of documentaries on this interesting period in English history.
c) The erection of memorials regarding the Battles.

12.4 The 52nd Oxfordshire Light Infantry Re-enactment & Research Group (1809)

www.52nd.org

The aim of this Group is to promote the Drill, conditions and atmosphere of the British Army of 1809. The Group intends to promote a strong camaraderie both internally and with other (external) re-enactment groups.

It is not to be confused with the Second World War re-enactor group of the same regiment. They are separate organisations and they consider different periods in time.

12.5 7th Battalion Royal Irish Rifles Re-enactors

www.geocities.com/Athens/Acropolis/2354/

This is the homepage of the 7th Battalion Royal Irish Rifles Re-enactors. They are the living history branch of the Great War Association (see Section 12.6). The site has colourful pictures and diagrams of the equipment and weapons that this unit's soldiers would have used.

The website has two main elements namely, (1) the re-enactment organisation and (2) a review of the British Army in World War 1. Both sections are informative and yield nuggets of information.

12.6 The Great War Association

www.great-war-assoc.org

The Great War is largely unknown to many Americans. The GWA strives to keep alive the history of the Great War and to honour those who participated in the conflict. The GWA does this through battle re-enactments and organising educational events. The GWA owns a 100-acre sight which has been used to authentically recreate a portion of the Western Front as it may have appeared in 1917–1918.

The battle re-enactments take place within a system of opposing trenches and a pock-marked no-man's land. There are the expected belts of barbed wire, sandbagged trenches and functioning machine guns. Behind the front lines there are communication and support trenches where the officers plan operations and the soldiers get something to eat and rest.

12.7 Oxfordshire and Buckinghamshire Light Infantry Re-enactors (WW2)

www.io.com/~tog/

The Oxfordshire and Buckinghamshire Light Infantry (OBLI) is a World War 2 "British" re-enacting group. It is headquartered in Austin, Texas, USA and the membership crosses the vast state. The organisation is dedicated to preserving the past through the collection and presentation of 1939 to 1945 uniforms, equipment and vehicles.

The OBLI travels to public events where they stage mock battles and assist in providing living history. They also stage war games and they work with other "Allied" and "Axis" re-enactment groups.

The website illustrates restoration projects for several jeeps and equipment; the fabrication of an operational Daimler Dingo scout car, and an outstanding collection of equipment and uniforms.

13 Miscellaneous

13.1 Bletchley Park

www.bletchleypark.org.uk

Bletchley Park, better known as "Station X", is where the world's first programmable computer and other technologies were initiated. Its formal name was "The National Codes Centre Bletchley Park". During WW2 the German armed forces' top secret codes were broken at Bletchley Park. This success provided the Allies with vital information that helped with the war effort. Located 50 miles north of London (near Milton Keynes), Bletchley Park was the host to a diverse range of code breakers including Dilly Knox and Alan Turing. Both the important Enigma and Lorenz codes were broken by the outstanding team. This work saved thousands of Allied servicemen's and servicewomen's lives.

The code breakers had to devise methods to break these extremely complex codes and their efforts enabled them to read decoded enemy messages within hours of their transmission by the enemy. Colossus, the world's first semi-programmable computer, was designed to break the Lorenz code which was used by the German High Command for their most secret communications.

13.2 Camp – X

http://webhome.idirect.com/~lhodgson/campx.htm

Camp X was a top secret World War 2 spy training school for the Allies. It was located on the shores of Lake Ontario in Canada and it was also known as Special Training School 103 (STS 103). Lynn Philip Hodgson has written a definitive account of the Camp called "Inside Camp-X" and this book covers the history of the school. Personnel from the secret services like Special Operations Executive (the UK's SOE), Secret Intelligence Service (the UK's MI6 / SIS) , Co-ordinator of Information (the USA's COI), Office of Strategic Services (the USA's OSS), Central Intelligence Agency (the USA's CIA) , British Security Co-ordination (the UK's BSC), Office of War Information (the USA's OWI) and the Federal Bureaux of Investigations (the USA's FBI) were trained at the Camp.

The website provides an interesting overview of the activities of Camp X and the key personnel. For those seeking more information on this little known facility the website provides an interesting starting point. It is possible to tour the site, see the facilities of STS 103 and visit the museum.

13.3 The Auxiliary Units or British Resistance Organisation of World War 2 (1940 - 1945)

http://warlinks.com/pages/auxiliary.html

This interesting site deals with the (British) civilian volunteers called the "Auxiliary Units". This was the innocuous codename for a resistance organisation. The aim was that if the UK was invaded these volunteers would conduct sabotage, spying and guerrilla warfare from behind the enemy lines. The force comprised of three main groups namely, (1) Fighting Patrols, (2) Special Duties and (3) Signals.

The Auxiliary Units were formed from primarily the Home Guard and operated from secret underground bases. Usually a patrol of six to eight men was lead by a sergeant and a local commander (a Lieutenant or Captain) coordinated regional activities.

The units were formed in three commands (GHQ Special Reserve Battalions). One for each of: (1) Scotland and the North, (2) The Midlands and (3) Southern Counties. The number of personnel involved totalled about 3,000. This site provides data on an interesting and little known military formation.

13.4 Voluntary Aid Detachments (VAD)
www.juroch.demon.co.uk/kentvad.htm
The Voluntary Aid Detachments were first formed in Kent during 1910. It was a scheme for groups of volunteers to support the medical services of the Territorial Force. This site deals with the Kent VAD but it provides a useful insight into the activities and duties of the VAD. The Kent VAD ran over 80 auxiliary military hospitals and nursed troops from Britain, Belgium, Australia and Canada.

The male volunteers in the VAD were often hospital orderlies and organised transport whilst the female staff planned hospitals and trained as nurses. The eighty or so hospitals run by the Kent VAD provided accommodation for around 4,730 patients and local surgeons / physicians provided advice and care for the injured. By the end of the war, the hospitals of the Kent VAD had handled 125,000 patients. This was the largest operation of its kind in the UK.

The Red Cross (see Section 7.7) helped in the administration and training of VAD units and it is worth noting that the Red Cross holds the personnel files for the VADs.

13.5 Angels and Orderlies (Military Hospital Staff During the Crimean War)
www.dorsetbay.plus.com/source/renkioilist.htm
These pages are a compilation of information on the individuals who served in the military hospitals during the Crimean War. The alphabetical list includes most of the British Nursing staff. The staff list, the "Renkioi List", is complete and information on other hospitals is being published as and when it becomes available.

13.6 The Edith Cavell Website
www.edithcavell.org.uk
Edith Cavell was a British nurse who cared for the sick and wounded on both sides of the First World War. She was committed to her work and stayed at Brussels after

the Germans had conquered Belgium. The clinic where she worked before the war became a Red Cross Hospital and most of the British nurses were sent home by the Germans.

During the autumn of 1914 two stranded British soldiers found their way into Nurse Cavell's training school and they were sheltered there for two weeks. Other soldiers soon followed and they were spirited away to neutral Holland. An underground network soon sprouted and Nurse Cavell was at the centre of it.

Edith Cavell faced a moral dilemma. Being a Red Cross nurse she should have remained impartial but she was prepared to sacrifice her conscience for the sake of her fellow countrymen. She helped save many allied soldiers but eventually her luck ran out and she was arrested by the Germans.

During her trial she freely admitted helping allied troops evade capture and she was sentenced to death by firing squad. She was executed on October 12th 1915 and the public outcry astounded the Germans. The execution was a propaganda coup for the British. It helped sway a neutral USA and aided recruitment of British troops which doubled for two weeks.

The site explores Nurse Cavell's life story in further details and provides light on the activities of nurse during this horrible conflict.

13.7 Shot at Dawn
www.shotatdawn.org.uk
This site deals with the subject of military executions during the First World War. Both sides of the conflict are considered. Rarely did the "prisoners" have the benefit of any legal representation or assistance whilst they were on trial for their lives. This subject is amazing but a very troubling one.

There are stories about the defendants' acts which lead to their untimely death. The narratives show how men lost their lives for relatively minor offences. Britain (including the Commonwealth) executed 346 of its soldiers, France 600 and Italy about 500.

13.8 Military Vehicle Preservation Association
www.mvpa.org
The MVPA was formed in 1976 with the aim of preserving military vehicles. It is a non-profit organisation based in the USA and has a worldwide membership. The MVPA is dedicated to fulfilling the needs of military vehicle enthusiasts, vehicle preservers and restorers, historians, collectors, shows and parades etc.

The MVPA publishes two journals called "Army Motors" and "Supply Line", and it holds an annual convention. The MVPA can supply technical advice regarding military vehicles and their preservation.

13.9 Military Heritage – Home of the Discriminating General

www.militaryheritage.com

The Military Heritage site is home to a company specialising in reproduction uniforms, swords and other items needed to equip personnel. Their target market is film making bodies and they have reproduction equipment for the Napoleonic wars, the American Revolution, the Seven Years War and British Army products for 1793 to 1856

They stock helmets, armour, buttons, belt plates, weapons, sword and sabres and equipment like drums and bugles. If you are seeking reproduction equipment for films, documentaries or re-enactment then this website is an ideal starting point.

13.10 Murphy's Register

www.harpers-online.com

Murphy's Register is an online database of photographs of service personnel who served in or around the Great War period. The sources include newspapers, school, university, business, town and county rolls of honour, regimental histories as well as Harpers own archives.

Harpers are active in the trading of militaria. If one follows the links to "Murphy's Register" one can access the database. It is possible to do online searches based on an individual's family name. This would result (if positive) in a list of possible matches and preliminary details to aid identification. These details include initials, first name(s), unit and rank. A second level of screening can be used and this is based upon attributable awards, date of death, commission date, ship(s) served (if appropriate) etc. If a match is made, it is possible to obtain a copy of the photograph for a small fee.

14 Internet Based Discussion Lists

The following is based upon known discussion lists. Each discussion list considers a specific topic and there are various levels of activity.

14.1 Australian Military History

This list is for the discussion and sharing of information on Australian military history and personnel. The period covered is from 1788 to the present day. To subscribe send an e-mail stating "subscribe" to aus-military-l-request@rootsweb.com.

14.2 Australian Imperial Forces 1914 – 1919

This is for anyone researching family members who served in the Australian Imperial Forces during the First World War. To subscribe send "subscribe" to aus-aif-i-request@rootsweb.com.

14.3 Australian Prisoners of War

Issues surrounding Australian POWs are examined here. To subscribe send an e-mail to australian-pows-l-request@roostweb.com.

14.4 Boer War

This is for those interested in the study and research into the Boer War. To subscribe send an e-mail stating "subscribe" to boer-war-l-request@rootsweb.com.

14.5 British Regiments

British and Indian Army Regiments are the focus of this list. Genealogy studies and unit histories are the principal topics. To subscribe send an e-mail stating "subscribe" to britregiments-subscribe@yahoogroups.com.

14.6 The Crimean War

The history of the Crimean War of 1854 – 1856 and genealogical data on participants are exchanged over this list. To subscribe send an e-mail stating "subscribe" to crimean-war-l-request@rootsweb.com.

14.7 The Great War

The discussion and sharing of information on the Great War is conducted via this discussion list. It is ideal for genealogical research and the history of formations. To subscribe send an e-mail stating "subscribe" to greatwar-l-request@rootsweb.com.

14.8 Korean War

This list handles research and genealogical studies regarding the Korean War in the1950s. To subscribe send and e-mail stating "subscribe" to Korean-war-l-request@rootsweb.com.

14.9 Napoleonic Wars
This list is suitable for those with an interest in Napoleonic studies such as the Peninsular Wars and Waterloo. To subscribe send an e-mail stating "subscribe" to napoleonic-l-request@rootsweb.com.

14.10 New Zealand Fencibles
The New Zealand Fencibles was a corps of retired soldiers who originated from the UK and Ireland. They formed a defence force to protect the early settlers in Auckland, Australia. The Fencibles arrived in Australia during 1847 to 1852 and the 2,500 men constituting the Fencibles arrived on various transport ships.
The New Zealand Fencibles has a website at *http://freepages.genealogy.rootsweb.com/~nzfencibles/* and the discussion list for them is available at new-zealand-fencibles-l-request@rootsweb.com. If you wish to subscribe to the mailing list send "subscribe" to the e-mail address.

14.11 New Zealand Military History
The military history of New Zealand and NZ military genealogy are discussed here. To subscribe send an e-mail to nz-military-l-request@rootsweb.com stating "subscribe".

14.12 Royal Australian Navy
This is for those which have a genealogical interest in the Royal Australian Navy. To subscribe send "subscribe" to aus-ran-l-request@roots.web.

14.13 Scottish Prisoners of War (In the 1600's)
Scottish prisoners of war taken by the English after the Battles of Dunbar (1650) and Worcester (1651) were sent to the British Colonies in North America and other island colonies. These Scots are now called the Scots Covenanter. The discussion list seeks to research issues related to these POWs. The goal of the list is to identify ships' lists, prisoner lists and other genealogical data relevant to these Scottish Rebels.
You can subscribe to the list by either *http://groups.yahoo.com/group/scottishwarprisoners/* or by sending the word "subscribe" to scottishwarprisoners-subscribe@yahoogroups.com.

14.14 Scottish Families after the Battle of Culloden
After the Battle of Culloden (in Scotland) there was the involuntary migration of many Scots in what was termed the Highland Clearances. This list discusses the issues surrounding these Scots. To subscribe send an e-mail stating "subscribe" to sct-highland-clearance-i-request@roots.web.

14.15 German Prisoner of War Camps (Stalags) in WW2

The issues surrounding the German run Stalags in WW2 (or POW camps) and the prisoners that were held in them are discussed here. To subscribe send an e-mail stating "subscribe" to stalag-pow-camps-l-request@rootsweb.com.

14.16 World War 2

This is a mailing list for those researching WW2, genealogy, the service records of WW2 personnel and WW2 units and formations. To subscribe send an e-mail stating "subscribe" to worldwar2-l-request@rootsweb.com.

Appendix A. Popular Internet Search Engines

Engine	URL[3]	Description
Altavista	*www.altavista.com*	Altavista is a fast and powerful search engine that indexes web content. They do not review or evaluate sites and the subject directory transfers you to http://uk.dir.yahoo.com.
		It has several complex but very helpful features, such as advanced syntax searching. This enables you to narrow and refine your search. This is important as Altavista will return lots of documents if the search criteria are too broad.
Yahoo	*http://uk.yahoo.com*	Yahoo is a subject based search engine, which catalogues websites according to their content. It is not only a search engine but a directory as well.
		Yahoo reviews sites and uses a hierarchical structure to index them. If you have a subject in mind you can use the directory part of the site.
Lycos	*www.lycos.com*	Lycos' main feature is a fast trawl of the internet. It used to provide an excellent directory service but now that has been replaced by an efficient search mechanism for people, Yellow Pages, shopping etc.
Hotbot	*www.hotbot.com*	Currently, Hotbot appears to use the functionality of the "Ask Jeeves" and "Google" search engines rather than its own technology. Both of these engines are very powerful.
Ask Jeeves	*http://uk.ask.com*	Ask Jeeves is a search engine of search engines with the added capability of understanding questions in plain English. Ask Jeeves has been created to utilise the knowledge of real human researchers.
		Ask Jeeves searches its own extensive knowledge / data base and passes your question to other popular search engines such as those in this list.
Google	*www.google.co.uk*	Google is a popular search engine and it currently offers various additional services. It is primarily a search engine and does not have a directory based listing.
		It does offer translation facilities for those foreign language documents.

---

[3] URL stands for Uniform Resource Locator. This is the internet address of a specific site.

Appendix B. Regimental Rosters and Histories

Below is a list of websites dealing with Regimental or Unit histories. The list is not exhaustive and there may be sites other than those listed below. Some of the sites are the official site for the unit and others are privately organised.

The official sites for each regiment can be found at
http://www.army.mod.uk/unitsandorgs/regiments_battalions.htm

In addition, many regiments also have their own site. The following list is based upon a number of sources and includes data obtained from *www.cyndislist.com.*

Regiment	Comments	Regimental Website
1st, The Queen's Dragoon Guards		*www.qdg.org.uk*
5th Norfolk, The Sandringham Battalion	Commonly called "The Lost Battalion" and raised from the Royal Estate at Sandringham.	*http://user.glo.be/~snelders/ sand.htm*
5th, The Royal Irish Lancers		*www.royalirishlancers.co.uk*
10th Lincolns, The Grimsby Chums		*www.eebo.freeserve.co.uk/ch ums.htm*
16th, The Irish Division		*http://freespace.vigin.net/sh. k/xvidiv.html*
22nd, The (Cheshire) Regiment		*http://web.ukonline.co.uk/ew h.bryan/Cheshire-1.htm*
41st, The Regiment of Foot	Gives details of deserters and / or settlers in North America	*http://freepages.history.roots web.com/~british41st/41stre gt_deserters.htm*
58th Foot (Rutlandshire) Regiment	Covers dates 1844 - 1847	*http://freepages.history.roots web.com/~garter1/58thfoot. htm*
76th Regiment of Foot	Brief history of the regiment from 1787 to 1870.	*http://members.ozemail.com. au/~clday/76foot.htm*
Ayrshire Rifle Volunteers	Online scans of Company Muster Rolls for the Maybole Company.	*www.maybole.org/history/Ar chives/rifle/volunteers.htm*
Birmingham Pals, The		*www.birminghampals.co.uk*
Black Watch, The		*www.army.mod.uk/blackwat ch/*
British and Indian Armies	Covers the nineteenth century.	*www.members.dca.net/fbl/*

Regiment	Comments	Regimental Website
British Light Infantry Regiments	Includes Duke of Cornwall's, Somerset, Durham, King's Own Yorkshire, Herefordshire, Ox and Bucks and Perthshire Volunteers	*www.lightinfantry.org.uk*
Cambridgeshire Regiment, The		*www.rootsweb.com/~engca m/Military/cambregt.htm*
Cheshire Regiment, The		*www.cheshireregiment.org.u k*
Chesterfield Sherwood's	Refers to the Somme (WW1) offensive	*http://homepage.ntlworld.co m/mike.briggs76/*
Duke of Edinburgh's Royal Regiment, The (Berkshire and Wiltshire)	Covers 49th, 62nd, 66th, & 99th Foot.	*www.farmerboys.com*
Glorious Glosters, The		*http://members.tripod.com/ %7EGlosters/index.html*
Green Howards, The	Alexandra, Princess of Wales's Own Yorkshire Regiment & the 19th Regiment of Foot.	*www.army.mod.uk/greenho wards/index.html*
Huntingdonshire Cyclist Battalions		*www.huntscycles.co.uk*
Oxfordshire and Buckinghamshire Light Infantry 43rd and 52nd Regiment of Foot.		*www.warpath.orbat.com/reg ts/ox_bucks.htm* *www.regimental-art.com/ox_and_bucks_light _inf.htm* *www.lightinfantry.org.uk*
Queen's Lancashire Regiment, The		*www.army.mod.uk/qlr/index. htm*
Royal East Kent Regiment, The (The Buff's)		*www.digiserve.com/peter/bu ffs/*
Royal Gloucestershire Hussars, The		*http://freepages.genealogy.r ootsweb.com/~terryw/glouce st/gloucest.htm#_The_Royal _Gloucestershire_2*
Royal Hampshire Regiment, The	A history of the Royal Hampshire Regiment from 1702 - 1992.	*www.pauljerrard.com*
Royal Lancashire Volunteers, The	An index of 661 men, mainly from Lancashire, who were recruited during the late 18th century.	*www.gmcro.co.uk/sources/m index.htm*
Royal Northumberland Fusiliers, The		*www.northumberlandfusilier s.org.uk*

Regiment	Comments	Regimental Website
Scottish Regiments in the Commonwealth		*www.btinternet.com/~james. mckay/commonwr.htm*
Sheffield City Battalion, The		*www.pals.org.uk/sheffield/*
Sherwood Foresters Regiment, The	Contains a history of the regiment.	*http://freespace.virgin.net/st ephen.mee/index.htm*
Singapore Volunteer Corps, The Eurasian Company	Some biographical details and photographs of personnel of a militia company formed by the British Military at Singapore in the late 19th and early 20th century. Alphabetical list of SVC members, where available, from inception until commencement of Japanese Occupation, 15 Feb 1942.	*http://home.ozconnect.net/tfo en/eurasiansvc.htm*
Somerset & Cornwall Light Infantry		*www.lightinfantry.org.uk*
Suffolk Regt., The	Considers the 11th Battalion	*www.curme.co.uk/102.htm*
Tyneside Scottish and Tyneside Irish Brigades		*www.tyneside-scottish.co.uk*

Appendix C. Regimental Associations on the Internet

Regiment, Corps or Formation	Internet Site Address
Adjutant General's Corps Regimental Association	*www.agcorps.org*
Airborne Forces Security Fund	*http://www.army.mod.uk/para/the_parachute_regimental_association/index.htm* and *www.army.mod.uk/para/airborne_forces_security_fund/index.htm*
Argyll and Sutherland Highlanders	*www.argylls.co.uk*
Army Air Corps Association	*www.aaca.org.uk*
Army Catering Corps Association	*www.accassociation.org*
Army Physical Training Corps Association	*www.aptc.org.uk/association_page.htm*
Black Watch Association	*www.theblackwatch.co.uk/assoc/index.html*
Coldstream Guards Association	*www.army.mod.uk/coldstreamguards/coldstream_guards_association.htm*
Devonshire and Dorset Regiment Association	*www.army.mod.uk/ddli/the_regimental_association/index.htm*
First Aid Nursing Yeomanry (FANY)	*www.fany.org.uk*
Fusiliers Regimental Aid Society	*www.army.mod.uk/fusiliers/regimental_aid.htm*
Green Howards', The Friends of	*www.greenhowards.org.uk*
Grenadier Guards Association	*www.grenadierguardsassn.freeserve.co.uk*
Intelligence Corps Association	*www.army.mod.uk/intelligencecrops/ica*
Irish Guards Association	*www.army.mod.uk/irishguards/association/index.htm*
King's Royal Hussars Welfare Fund	*www.krh.org.uk*
The Lovat Scouts Regimental Association	*www.qohldrs.co.uk/html/about_us.htm*
Princess of Wales's Royal Regiment (Queen's and Royal Hampshires) Regimental Association and Benevolent Fund	*www.pwrr-army.co.uk*
1st Queen's Dragoon Guards Regimental Association	*www.qdg.org.uk*
Queen's Own Cameron Highlanders Regimental Association & Queen's Own	*www.qohldrs.co.uk*
Queen's Royal Hussars Benevolent Fund	*www.qrh.org.uk*
Queen's Royal Lancers Regimental Association	*www.qrl.uk.com*
Queen's Royal Surrey Regiment Regimental Association	*www.queensregiment.com*
Royal Army Educational Corps Association	*www.agc-ets.co.uk*
Royal Army Medical Corps Charitable Fund 1992	*www.army.mod.uk/medical/royal_army_medical_corps/ramc_association/index.htm*
Royal Army Ordnance Corps Charitable Trust	*www.army-rlc.co.uk*

Regiment, Corps or Formation	Internet Site Address
Royal Army Pay Corps Regimental Association	*www.rapc.co.uk*
Royal Army Service Corps and Royal Corps of Transport Association and Benevolent Fund	*www.waggoners.co.uk/wbsitepages/rctassoc.htm*
Royal Engineers Association	*www.reahq.org.uk*
Royal Fusiliers Society	*http://www.army.mod.uk/fusiliers/associations/index.htm*
Royal Gloucestershire, Berkshire and Wiltshire Regimental Association	*www.glosters.org*
Royal Highland Fusiliers Regimental Benevolent Association	*www.rhf.org.uk*
9th/12th Royal Lancers (Prince of Wales's) Regimental Association	*www.spearman.fsbusiness.co.uk/association.htm*
Royal Logistic Corps Regimental Association	*www.army-rlc.co.uk*
Royal Pioneer Corps Association	*www.royalpioneercorps.co.uk*
Royal Signals Association	*www.army.mod.uk/royalsignals/rsa/*
Royal Scots Dragoon Guards Association	*www.scotsdg.com* and *www.army.mod.uk/scotsdg/*
Royal Sussex Regimental Association	*www.eastbournemuseums.co.uk*
Scots Guards Association	*www.scots-guards.co.uk*
Wessex (43rd) Association	*www.lightinfantry.org.uk/Regiments/43rd%20Wessex%20Association/43_index.htm*
Women's Royal Army Corps Association	*www.wracassociation.co.uk*
Worcestershire and Sherwood Foresters Regiment Welfare and General Charitable Fund	*www.wfr.org.uk*

Appendix D. Summary of Campaigns and Conflicts Involving the British Army

The following list is a summary of campaigns and conflicts that have involved the British Army. It is not a complete list but covers the more famous ones.

Source: The National Army Museum (*www.national-army-museum.ac.uk*)

Campaigns List
The English Civil War
Glorious Revolution
War of the Spanish Succession
The Jacobite Risings
The War of the Austrian Succession
The Seven Years War
The American War of Independence

Nineteenth Century
The Road to Waterloo
      The British Army 1793-1815
Peninsular War
Waterloo
Afghan Wars
First China War
Sikh Wars
Crimean War
      Charge of the Light Brigade
Indian Mutiny
Ashanti Wars
Zulu War
Egypt and the Sudan
North West Frontier
Boer War

First World War 1914 -1918
Mons to Ypres
East Africa
Mesopotamia
Gallipoli

First World War 1914 -1918 (Contd)
Salonika
Darfur
Palestine
Battle of the Somme

Second World War 1939-1945
The Fall of France
The Far East Campaign
North Africa
Italy
North West Europe

Post-War Conflicts
Palestine
Indian Partition
Malaya
Korea
Kenya
Cyprus
Egypt – The Canal Zone
Suez
Borneo
Aden
Northern Ireland
Falklands
Gulf War (1st)
Bosnia
Kosovo
Sierra Leone
NATO Operations
Gulf War (2nd)

Appendix E.   Regimental Collections by Museum

The following data is based upon research conducted by the author and data on the Army Museums Ogilby Trust's website (see *www.armymuseums.co.uk*). The table refers to the museum(s) that hold the collection(s) for the various units, regiments etc of the army. The list contains all known collections. Historical names and unit numbers are included. However, not all historic regiments and formations are covered. Thus, it is not exhaustive for every unit and / or formations that have existed within the British Army.

It is important to note that units whose name is prefixed by Colonel, Duke, Earl, Sir etc are listed under the title holder's surname e.g. "Colonel Long's Regiment of Foot" is indexed under "Long's (Colonel) Regiment of Foot". The only exceptions to this are the titles of Royalty (e.g. Alexandra, Princess of Wales's Own Regiment of Yorkshire).

Museum Reference Numbers and Contact Details

Ref No.	Museum Name	Internet Addresses	Postal Address
1	101 (Northumbrian) Regiment Royal Artillery (Volunteers) Museum, Gateshead	No known website	Napier Armoury, Alexandra Rd, Gateshead, Tyne & Wear, NE8 4HX
2	13th / 18th Royal Hussars and the Light Dragoons Museum	*http://lightdragoons.org .uk*	Cannon Hall, Cawthorne, Barnsley, South Yorkshire, S75 4AT
3	Museum of Lancashire [4]	*www.lancashire.gov.uk* (see Education Dept) *www.krh.org.uk* *www.1420h.org.uk*	Stanley Street, Preston, Lancashire, PR1 4YP
4	Soldier's Life, Discovery Museum	*www.lightdragoons.org. uk*	Blandford Sq, Newcastle-upon-Tyne, Tyne & Wear, NE1 4JA
5	1st The Queen's Dragoon Guards Museum	*www.qdg.org.uk*	Cardiff Castle, Castle St, Cardiff, South Glamorgan, CF10 2RB

---

[4] The Museum of Lancashire referred the author to all three of these sites as they all consider the museum.

Ref No.	Museum Name	Internet Addresses	Postal Address
6	Wilberforce House Museum	No known website but see *www.hullcc.gov.uk*	Ferens Art Gallery, Queen Victoria Sq, Hull, Kingston-upon-Hull, HU1 3RA
7	Derby Museum and Art Gallery	*www.derby.gov.uk/muse ums*	The Strand, Derby, Debyshire, DE1 1BS
8	Adjutant General's Corps (AGC) Museum Collection	No known website	The Guardroom, Peninsula Barracks, Romsey Rd, Winchester, Hampshire, SO23 8TS
9	Airborne Forces Museum, Aldershot	*www.army.mod.uk/para /af_museum*	Browning Barracks, Aldershot, Hampshire, GU11 2BU
10	Aldershot Military Museum	*www.hants.gov.uk/muse um/aldershot*	Queen's Av., Aldershot, Hampshire, GU11 2LG
11	Argyll and Sutherland Highlanders Regimental Museum, Stirling	*www.argylls.co.uk*	The Castle, Stirling, Scotland, FK8 1EH
12	Army Medical Services Museum	*www.ams-museum.org.uk*	Keogh Barracks, Ash Vale, Aldershot, Hampshire, GU12 5RQ
13	Army Physical Training Corps Museum	*www.aptc.org.uk*	Army School of PT, Fox Lines, Queen's Av, Aldershot, Hampshire, GU11 2LB
14	Ayrshire Yeomanry Museum	No known website	Rozelle House Galleries, Monument Rd, Ayr, Ayrshire, Scotland, KA7 4NQ
15	Bank of England Museum	*www.bankofengland.co. uk/museum*	Bank of England Volunteers Collection, Threadneedle St, London, EC2R 8AH
16	Luton Museum and Art Gallery	*www.luton.gov.uk*	Bedfordshire & Hertfordshire Regt Museum Collection, Luton Museum & Art Gallery, Wardown Park, Luton, Bedfordshire, LU2 7HA

Ref No.	Museum Name	Internet Addresses	Postal Address
17	Berkshire and Westminster Dragoons Museum	No known website	Duke of York's Headquarters, King's Rd, London, SW3 4SC
18	Black Watch (Royal Highland Regiment) Regimental Museum	*www.theblackwatch.co.uk*	Balhousie Castle, Hay St, Perth, Perthshire, Scotland, PH1 5HR
19	Old Gaol Museum, Buckingham	*www.mkhertitage.co.uk/ogb/*	Buckinghamshire Military Museum Trust Collection, The Old Gaol Museum, Market Hill, Buckingham, Bedfordshire, MK18 1JX
20	Royal Museum and Art Gallery, Canterbury[5]	*www.canterbury-museums.co.uk*	Buffs, Royal East Kent Regt Museum Collection, 18 High St, Canterbury, Kent, CT1 2RA
21	The Old Gaol Museum, Ely [6]	*www.elymuseum.org.uk*	Ely Museum, The Old Gaol, Market St, Ely, Cambridgeshire, CB7 4LS
22	Low Parks Museum	*www.southlanarkshire.gov.uk*	Cameronians (Scottish Rifles) Museum Collection, Low Parks Museum, 129 Muir St, Hamilton, South Lanarkshire, Scotland, ML3 6BJ
23	Carmarthenshire County Museum	*www.carmarthenshire.gov.uk*	Carmarthen Militia and Volunteers Collection, Abergwili, Carmarthen, Carmarthenshire, Wales, SA31 2JG
24	Tenby Museum and Art Gallery	No known website	Castlemartin Yeomanry Museum Collection, Castle Hill, Tenby, Pembrokeshire, Wales, SA70 7BP

---

[5] There are still displays in Canterbury but the ownership of the collection and the archive has been transferred to the National Army Museum (www.national-army-museum.ac.uk).
[6] Some of the Cambridgeshire Regiment's artefacts are at the Old Gaol Museum, Ely and the remainder are at the Imperial War Museum Duxford.

Ref No.	Museum Name	Internet Addresses	Postal Address
25	Cheshire Military Museum	*www.chester.ac.uk/milit arymuseum*	The Castle, Chester, Cheshire, CH1 2DN
26	Duke of Cornwall's Light Infantry Museum	No known website	The Keep, Bodmin, Cornwall, PL31 1EG
27	Bankfield Museum	*www.dukes.org.uk*	Duke of Wellington's Regt (West Riding) Museum, Boothtown Rd, Halifax, West Yorkshire, HX3 6HG
28	Durham Light Infantry Museum & Durham Art Gallery	*www.durham.gov.uk/dli*	Aykley Heads, Durham City, Co Durham, DH1 5TU
29	Museum of Army Transport [7]	No known website	Flemingate, Beverley, North Humberside
30	Essex Regiment Museum	*www.chelmsford.gov.uk* Then follow links for "Museums".	Oaklands Park, Moulsham St, Chelmsford, Essex, CM2 9AQ
31	Essex Yeomanry Museum Collection	*www.essex-yeomanry.org.uk*	Springfield Lyons TA Centre, Colchester Rd, Chelmsford, Essex, CH2 5TA
32	Fife and Forfar Yeomanry Museum	No known website for the museum but try *www.army.mod.uk/qoy/ c-squadron/index.htm*	Yeomanry House, Castlebank Rd, Cupar, Fife, Scotland, KY15 4BL
33	Firepower! Museum of the Royal Artillery & Museum of Artillery at the Rotunda	*www.firepower.org.uk*	Royal Arsenal, Woolwich, London, SE18 6ST
34	Fusiliers' London Volunteers Museum	No known website	213 Balham High Rd, London, SW17 7BQ
35	Glamorgan Artillery Volunteers Museum	No known website	Raglan Barracks, Newport, Wales

---

[7] It is believed that the Museum of Army Transport held the "East Riding of Yorkshire Yeomanry Collection". According to the National Army Museum's website it appears that the Museum of Army Transport closed down shortly after August 2003. The collection of objects constituting the "East Riding of Yorkshire Yeomanry Collection" is now split between the Halifax Barracks in Hull and the Imphal Barracks at York (Museum reference 57). Further information can be gained from "East Riding of Yorkshire Yeomanry Collection, c/o Mr J Pollock, 47 Minster Av, Beverley, Yorkshire, HU17 0NL".

Ref No.	Museum Name	Internet Addresses	Postal Address
36	Gordon Highlanders Museum	www.gordonhighlanders.com	St Luke's, Viewfield Rd, Aberdeen, Aberdeenshire, Scotland, AB15 7XH
37	Green Howards Regimental Museum	www.greenhowards.org.uk	Trinity Church Sq, Richmond, North Yorkshire, DL10 4QN
38	Guards Museum	www.theguardsmuseum.com	Wellington Barracks, Birdcage Walk, London, SW1E 6HQ
39	Gurkha Museum	www.thegurkhamuseum.co.uk	Peninsula Barracks, Romsey Rd, Winchester, Hampshire, SO23 8TS
40	Herefordshire Regiment Museum	No known website	TA Centre, Harold St, Hereford, Herefordshire, HR1 2QX
41	Hertford Museum	www.hertford.net/museum/	Hertfordshire Regiment Museum Collection, 18 Bull Plain, Hertford, Hertfordshire, SG14 1DT
42	Hitchin Museum	No known website but www.north-herts.gov.uk has a few details.	Hertfordshire Yeomanry & Artillery Collection, Paynes Park, Hitchin, Hertfordshire, SG5 1EQ
43	Honourable Artillery Company Museum	www.hac.uk.com	Armoury House, City Rd, London, EC1Y 2BQ
44	Household Cavalry Museum	www.householdcavalry.co.uk	Combermere Barracks, St Leonards Rd, Windsor, Berkshire, SL4 3DN
45	Infantry and Small Arms School Corps Weapons Collection	No known website	HQ SASC, HQ Infantry Warminster Training Centre, Warminster, Wiltshire, BA12 0DJ
46	Inns of Court and City Yeomanry Museum	No known website	10 Stone Buildings, Lincoln's Inn, London, WC2A 3TG
47	Military Intelligence Museum	www.army.mod.uk/intelligencecorps/chicksands.htm	DISC Chicksands, Shefford, Bedfordshire, SG17 5PR
48	Jersey Militia Museum Collection	www.jerseyheritagetrust.org	Elizabeth Castle, St Aubin's Bay, St Helier, Jersey

Ref No.	Museum Name	Internet Addresses	Postal Address
49	The Devonshire and Dorset Regiment Museum	*www.keepmilitarymuseum.org*	The Keep, Bridport Rd, Dorchester, Dorset, DT1 1RN
50	Kent and Sharpshooters Yeomanry Museum	*www.ksymuseum.org.uk*	Hever Castle, Edenbridge, Kent, TN8 7NG
51	King's Own Royal Border Regiment Museum	*www.borderregimentmuseum.co.uk*	Queen Mary's Tower, The Castle, Carlisle, Cumbria, CA3 8UR
52	The King's Own Royal Regiment Museum	*www.kingsownmuseum.plus.com*	City Museum, Market Sq, Lancaster, Lancashire, LA1 1HT
53	King's Own Scottish Borderers Regimental Museum	*www.kosb.co.uk*	The Barracks, Berwick-upon-Tweed, Northumberland, TD15 1DG
54	Doncaster Museum and Art Gallery	*www.doncaster.gov.uk*	King's Own Yorkshire Light Infantry Museum Collection, Chequer Rd, Doncaster, South Yorkshire, DN1 2AE
55	Museum of Liverpool Life	*www.nmgm.org.uk/liverpoollife/galleries.asp*	King's Regiment Museum Collection, Pier Head, Liverpool, L3 1PZ
56	The King's Royal Hussars Museum in Winchester	*www.hants.gov.uk/leisure/museum/royalhus*	Peninsula Barracks, Romsey Rd, Winchester, Hampshire, SO23 8TS
57	Kohima (2nd Division) Museum	No known website	Imphal Barracks, Fulford Rd, York, YO10 4AU
58	Leeds Rifles Museum Collection	No known website	c/o 7 Wentworth Court, Rastrick, Brighouse, West Yorkshire, HD6 3XD
59	Leicestershire Yeomanry Museum Collection	No known website	The War Memorial Museum, Queen's Park, Loughborough, Leicestershire, LE11 2TT
60	Light Infantry Museum (Winchester)	*www.winchestermilitarymuseums.co.uk*	Peninsula Barracks, Romsey Rd, Winchester, Hampshire, SO23 8TS

Ref No.	Museum Name	Internet Addresses	Postal Address
61	Museum of Lincolnshire Life	*www.lincolnshire.gov.uk/museumoflincolnshirelife*	Lincolnshire Yeomanry Museum, Burton Rd, Lincoln, Lincolnshire, LN1 3LY
62	Liverpool Scottish Regimental Museum	*www.liverpoolscottish.org.uk*	c/o 51a Common Lane, Culcheth, Warrington, Liverpool, WA3 4EY
63	London Irish Rifles Museum	No known website	Duke of York's Headquarters, King's Rd, London, SW3 4SA
64	London Scottish Regiment Museum	*www.londonscottishregt.org/museum.cfm*	95 Horseferry Rd, London, SW1P 2DX
65	Manchester Regiment Museum	*www.tameside.gov.uk*	The Town Hall, Market Place, Ashton-under-Lyne, Tameside, OL6 6DL
66	Manx Regiment Museum	*www.iomguide.com/douglas/regimental-museum.php* This museum is currently moving to the "Aviation and Military Museum" see *www.iomguide.com/aviationmilitarymuseum.php*	MacClellan Hall, Tromode Rd, Douglas, Isle of Man, IM4 3LL
67	Powysland Museum	See *http://powysmuseums.powys.gov.uk* for the	Montgomeryshire Yeomanry Museum Collection The Canal Wharf, Welshpool, Powys, Wales, SY21 7AQ
68	Museum of Army Chaplaincy	*www.army.mod.uk/chaps/museum/index.htm*	Armed Forces Chaplaincy Centre, Amport House, Andover, Hampshire, SP11 8BG
69	Museum of Army Flying	*www.flying-museum.org.uk*	Middle Wallop, Stockbridge, Hampshire, SO20 8DY
70	National Army Museum	*www.national-army-museum.ac.uk*	Royal Hospital Rd, Chelsea, London, SW3 4HT

Ref No.	Museum Name	Internet Addresses	Postal Address
71	North Irish Horse Regimental Collection	No known website[8]	c/o Ballybogey House, Ballybogey, Co Antrim, Northern Ireland, BT53 6NS
72	Abington Museum	www.northampton.gov.uk/museums	Northamptonshire Regiment Museum Collection, Abington Park, Northampton, Northamtonshire, NN1 4LW
73	Oxfordshire and Buckinghamshire Light Infantry Museum	No known website[9]	Slade Park TA Barracks, Headington, Oxford, Oxfordshire, OX3 7JJ
74	Pembroke Yeomanry Collection	No known website	Scolton Manor Museum, Spittal, Haverfordwest, Pembrokeshire, Wales, SA62 5QL
75	Prince of Wales's Own Regiment of Yorkshire Regimental Museum	www.yorkshireregiment.mod.uk	3 Tower St, York, Yorkshire, YO1 9SB
76	Princess Louise's Kensington Regiment Museum	No known website	41 (PLK) Signals Squadron (V), TAC Marlpit Lane, Coulsdon, Surrey
77	Princess of Wales's Royal Regiment and Queen's Regiment Museum	www.army.mod.uk/pwrr/	5 Keep Yard, Dover Castle, Dover, Kent, CT16 1HU
78	Queen's Lancashire Regiment Museum	www.army.mod.uk/qlr/museum_archives/index.htm	Fulwood Barracks, Watling Street Rd, Preston, Lancashire, PR2 8AA
79	Queen's Own Highlanders Museum Collection	www.scottishmuseums.org.uk	Fort George, Ardersier, Invernessshire, Scotland, IV2 3XD

---

[8] The artefacts of this museum are held in the TA Centre at Dunmore Park Estate in Belfast but the collection is not open to the public.
[9] The Oxfordshire and Buckinghamshire Light Infantry (OBLI) do not have a website. The Soldiers of Oxfordshire (SOFO) is a trust which exists with the purpose of creating a military museum in Oxfordshire. Other participating organisations are the Oxfordshire Yeomanry and the Oxford University Officers Training Corps. The SOFO has a rudimentary website at www.sofo.org.uk.

Ref No.	Museum Name	Internet Addresses	Postal Address
80	Queen's Own Hussars Museum	www.qohmuseum.org.uk	Lord Leycester Hospital. High St, Warwick, Warwickshire, CV34 4BH
81	Queen's Own Mercian Yeomanry Museum	No known website	Bridgeman House, Cavan Drive, Cemetery Road, Dawley, Telford TF4 2BQ
82	Maidstone Museum and Art Gallery	www.museum.maidstone.gov.uk	Queen's Own Royal West Kent Regiment Museum Collection, St Faith's St, Maidstone, Kent, ME1 1LH
83	Queen's Royal Irish Hussars Museum Collection	www.eastbournemuseums.co.uk	Redoubt Fortress, Royal Parade, Eastbourne, East Sussex, BN22 7AQ
84	Queen's Royal Lancers Museum	www.qrl.uk.com	Belvoir Castle, Belvoir, Grantham, Lincolnshire, NG32 1PD
85	Queen's Royal Surrey Regiment Museum	www.queensroyalsurreys.org.uk	Clandon Park, Guildford, Surrey, GU4 7RQ
86	Royal Anglian Regiment and Cambridgeshire Regiment Collection10	www.royalanglianmuseum.org.uk	Land Warfare Hall, Imperial War Museum Duxford, Cambridge, Cambridgeshire, CB2 4QR
87	Royal Electrical & Mechanical Engineers Museum of Technology	www.rememuseum.org.uk	Isaac Newton Rd, Arborfield, Reading, Berkshire, RG2 9NJ
88	Royal Berkshire Yeomanry Cavalry Museum[11]	www.army.mod.uk/royalsignals/94sigsqn.htm www.berkshiremuseums.org.uk	TA Centre, Bolton Rd, Windsor, Berkshire, Sl4 3JG
89	Royal Devon Yeomanry Museum Collection	www.devonmuseums.net	Museum of Barnstaple and North Devon, The Square, Barnstaple, Devon, EX32 8LN

---

[10] Some elements of the Cambridgeshire Regiment Collection are at the Imperial War Museum Duxford and the remainder are at the Old Gaol Museum, Ely.

[11] The Royal Berkshire Yeomanry Cavalry Museum currently does not have it own website. However, they plan to develop one and details about the museum can be found on those listed above.

| --- | --- | --- | --- |
90	Royal Dragoon Guards Museum	www.rdgmuseum.org.uk	3 Tower St, York, Yorkshire, YO1 9SB
91	Royal Engineers Museum	www.royalengineers.org.uk	Brompton Barracks, Prince Arthur Rd, Gillingham, Kent, ME4 4UG
92	Royal Gloucestershire, Berkshire and Wiltshire Regiment Salisbury Museum	www.thewardrobe.org.uk	The Wardrobe, 58 The Close, Salisbury, Wiltshire, SP1 2EX
93	Royal Green Jackets Museum	www.royalgreenjackets.co.uk	Peninsula Barracks, Romsey Rd, Winchester, Hampshire, SO23 8TS
94	Royal Guernsey Militia Collection	www.museum.guernsey.net	Castle Cornet, St Peter Port, Guernsey
95	Royal Hampshire Regiment Museum	www.RoyalHampshireRegimentMuseum.co.uk	Serle's House, Southgate St, Winchester, Hampshire, SO23 9EG
96	Royal Highland Fusiliers Museum	www.rhf.org.uk	518 Sauchiehall St, Glasgow, Scotland, G2 3LW
97	Royal Hospital Museum	www.chelsea-pensioners.co.uk	Royal Hospital Chelsea, Royal Hospital Rd, London, SW3 4SR
98	Royal Inniskilling Fusiliers Regimental Museum	www.inniskilling.com	The Castle, Enniskillen, Co Fermanagh, Northern Ireland, BT74 7HL
99	Royal Irish Fusiliers Regimental Museum	www.rirfus-museum.freeserve.co.uk	Sovereign's House, The Mall, Armagh, Co Armagh, Northern Ireland, BT61 9DI
100	Royal Irish Regiment Museum	www.royalirishregiment.co.uk	St Patrick's Barracks, Ballymena, Co Antrim, Northern Ireland, BT43 7BH
101	Royal Leicestershire Regiment Museum Collection	www.leicester.gov.uk/museums	Newarke Houses Museum, The Newarke, Leicester, Leicestershire, LE2 7BY
102	Royal Logistic Corps Museum	www.army-rlc.co.uk	Princess Royal Barracks, Deepcut, Camberley, Surrey, GU16 6RW

Ref No.	Museum Name	Internet Addresses	Postal Address
103	Royal Military Academy Sandhurst Collection	No known website	Royal Military Academy Sandhurst, Camberley, Surrey, GU15 4PQ
104	Royal Military Police Museum	www.rhqrmp.freeserve.co.uk	Roussillon Barracks, Broyle Rd, Chichester, West Sussex, PO19 4BN
105	Royal Military School of Music Museum	No known website	Kneller Hall, Twickenham, Middlesex, TW2 7DU
106	Royal Monmouthshire Royal Engineers (Militia) Museum Collection	www.monmouthcastlemuseum.org.uk	Castle and Regimental Museum, The Castle, Monmouth, Monmouthshire, Wales, NP25 3BS
107	Royal Norfolk Regimental Museum	www.rnrm.org.uk	Shirehall Market Avenue, Norwich, Norfolk, NR1 3JQ
108	Fusiliers' Museum, Lancashire	www.fusiliersmuseum-lancashire.org.uk	Wellington Barracks, Bolton Rd, Bury, Lancashire, BL8 2PL
109	Royal Regiment of Fusiliers (London) Museum	No known website	HM Tower of London, London, EC3N 4AB
110	Royal Regiment of Fusiliers (Northumberland) Museum	www.northumberlandfusiliers.org.uk	The Abbott's Tower, Alnwick, Northumberland, NE66 1NG
111	Royal Regiment of Fusiliers (Royal Warwickshire) Museum	www.warwickfusiliers.co.uk	St John's House, Warwick, Warwickshire, CV34 4NF
112	Royal Scots Dragoon Guards Museum	www.theroyalscots.co.uk	The Castle, Edinburgh, Scotland, EH1 2YT
113	Royal Scots Regimental Museum	www.theroyalscots.co.uk	The Castle, Edinburgh, Scotland, EH1 2YT
114	Royal Signals Museum	www.royalsignalsmuseum.com	Blandford Camp, Blandford Forum, Dorset, DT11 8RH
115	Royal Ulster Rifles Museum	www.geocities.com/rurmusuem/	(83rd, 86th Royal Irish Rifles), 5 Waring St, Belfast, Northern Ireland, BT1 2EW

Ref No.	Museum Name	Internet Addresses	Postal Address
116	Royal Welch Fusiliers Museum	*www.rwfmuseum.org.uk*	The Castle, Caernarfon, Gwynedd, Wales, LL55 2AY
117	Royal Wiltshire Yeomanry Collection	*www.yeomanry.co.uk*	A (RWY) Sqn Royal Yeomanry, Church Place, Swindon, Wiltshire, SN1 5EH
118	Rutland County Museum	*www.rutnet.co.uk*	Catmose St, Oakham, Rutland, LE15 6HW
119	The Sherwood Foresters (Notts & Derby Regt) Collection	*www.wfrmuseum.org.uk*	The Castle, Nottingham, Nottinghamshire, NG1 6EL
120	Sherwood Rangers Yeomanry Museum	*www.sherwood-rangers.org*	S (SRY) Sqn The Royal Yeomanry, Cavendish Drive, Carlton, Nottinghamshire, NG4 3DX
121	Shropshire Regimental Museum	*www.shrewsburymuseums.com/castle*	The Castle, Shrewsbury, Shropshire, SY1 2AT
122	Soldiers of Gloucestershire Museum	*www.glosters.org.uk*	Custom House, Gloucester Docks, Gloucester, Gloucestershire, GL1 2HE
123	Somerset Military Museum	*www.sommilmuseum.org.uk*	Somerset County Museum, Taunton Castle, Taunton, Somerset, TA1 4AA
124	South Nottinghamshire Hussars Yeomanry Museum	No known website	The TA Centre, Hucknall Lane, Bulwell, Nottingham, Nottinghamshire, NG6 8AQ
125	South Wales Borderers and Monmouthshire Regiment Museum	*www.rrw.org.uk*	The Barracks, Brecon, Powys, Wales, LD3 7EB
126	Staff College Museum	No known website	Slim Rd, Camberley, Surrey, GU15 4NP
127	Staffordshire Regiment Museum	*www.army.mod.uk/staffords/regimental_museum/index.htm*	Whittington Barracks, Lichfield, Staffordshire, WS14 9PY

Ref No.	Museum Name	Internet Addresses	Postal Address
128	Staffordshire Yeomanry Museum	www.stafford.gov.uk	The Ancient High House, Greengate St, Stafford, Staffordshire, ST16 2JA
129	Suffolk and Norfolk Yeomanry Collection	www.muckleburgh.co.uk[12]	The Muckleburgh Collection, Weybourne, Holt, Norfolk, NR25 7EG
130	Suffolk Regiment Museum	www.suffolkregiment.org	The Keep, Gibraltar Barracks, Newmarket Rd, Bury St Edmunds, Suffolk, IP33 3RN
131	Surrey & Sussex Yeomanry Museum	www.newhavenfort.org.uk	Newhaven Fort, Fort Rd, Newhaven, East Sussex, BN9 9DS
132	Tank Museum, Bovington	www.tankmuseum.co.uk	Bovington Camp, Bovington, Dorset, BH20 6JG
133	Warwickshire Yeomanry Museum	www.warwick-uk.co.uk/places-of-interest/yeomanry-museum.asp	The Court House, Jury St, Warwick, Warwickshire, CV34 4EW
134	Waterbeach Station Museum	No known website	Waterbeach Barracks, Waterbeach, Cambridgeshire, CB5 9PA
135	Welch Regiment Museum	www.rrw.org.uk	Black and Barbican Towers, The Castle, Cardiff, South Glamorgan, Wales, CF10 2RB
136	Westmorland and Cumberland Yeomanry Museum	No known website	Dalemain House, Penrith, Cumbria, CA11 0HB
137	Worcestershire Regiment Museum Collection	www.wfrmuseum.org.uk and www.worcestercitymuseums.org.uk	City Museum and Art Gallery, Foregate St, Worcester, Worcestershire, WR1 1DT

---

[12] This museum has a small regimental collection and the museum covers other aspects of military history.

Ref No.	Museum Name	Internet Addresses	Postal Address
138	York and Lancaster Regiment Museum	*www.rotherham.gov.uk*	Central Library and Arts Centre, Walker Place, Rotherham, South Yorkshire, S65 1JH
139	Hitchin Museum	*www.north-herts.gov.uk* Then type "Hitchin Museum"	Paynes Park, Hitchin, Hertfordshire, SG5 1EQ

Appendix F. Museums for Regiments and Formations

The following table relates Regimental names, numbered Regiments and Formations to the Museums that care for artefacts of that particular organisation. The Museum Numbers in the right hand column refer to the list of museums in the table above in Appendix E.

Numbered Regiments and Formations	Museum Number	Numbered Regiments and Formations	Museum Number
1st (Irish Establishment) or 'Blue' Irish Horse	90	2nd Assam Sebundy Corps (1839-1844)	39
1st (King's Royal) Light Dragoons	4	2nd Bengal European Light Cavalry (Honourable East India Company)	3
1st and 2nd Herts Artillery Batteries (1908-1914)	139		
1st East Anglian Regiment (Royal Norfolk and Suffolk)	86	2nd Bombay European Light Infantry (Honourable East India Company)	28
1st Green Jackets	93	2nd Bombay European Regiment of Foot (Honourable East India Company)	28
1st Hertfordshire Light Horse (1862-1879)	139		
1st King George V's Own Gurkha Rifles (The Malaun Regiment)	39	2nd British Infantry Division (1944)	57
1st King's Dragoon Guards	5	2nd Division	57
1st Life Guards	44	2nd Dragoon Guards (Queen's Bays)	5
1st or Grenadier Regiment of Foot Guards	38	2nd East Anglian Regiment (Duchess of Gloucester's Own Royal Lincolnshire and Northamptonshire)	86
1st or King's Regiment of Dragoon Guards	5		
1st or Royal Regiment of Foot	113	2nd European Regiment, Bombay Light Infantry (Honourable East India Company)	28
1st or The Royal Scots Regiment	113		
1st Regiment of Foot Guards	38	2nd Green Jackets (King's Royal Rifle Corps)	93
1st Regiment of Foot or Royal Scots	113	2nd King Edward VII's Own Gurkha Rifles (The Sirmoor Rifles)	39
1st The Queen's Dragoon Guards	5		
2nd (Queen's) Dragoon Guards	5	2nd Life Guards	44
		2nd Madras (Light Infantry) Regiment	54

Numbered Regiments and Formations	Museum Number	Numbered Regiments and Formations	Museum Number
2nd Madras European Regiment (Light Infantry) (Honourable East India Company)	54	3rd East Anglian Regiment	86
		3rd Foot (2nd Battalion) reconstituted as 61st Foot	122
2nd Nusseri Battalion (1815-1830)	39	3rd Green Jackets (Rifle Brigade)	93
2nd or 'Green' Irish Horse	90	3rd Irish Horse	112
2nd or Queen's Regiment of Dragoon Guards	5	3rd Kent Rifle Volunteers	82
		3rd King's Own Hussars	80
2nd Regiment of Irish Horse	90	3rd King's Own Light Dragoons	80
2nd Royal North British Dragoons	112	3rd King's Own regiment of Dragoons	80
3rd (Bengal European Light Infantry) Regiment (Honourable East India Company)	83	3rd Light Dragoons	84
		3rd Queen Alexandra's Own Gurkha Rifles	39
3rd (Bengal Light Infantry) Regiment	83	3rd Regiment of Dragoon Guards	112
3rd (East Kent, The Buffs) Regiment	20	3rd Regiment of Dragoons	80
		3rd Regiment of Foot Guards	38
3rd (Madras Infantry) Regiment (Honourable East India Company)	98	3rd Regiment of Horse (Peterborough's) Queen's Regiment of Horse	5
3rd (Madras) Regiment (Honourable east India Company)	98	4th (or King's Own) Regiment of Foot	52
3rd (or The Buffs) Regiment of Foot	20	4th (The King's Own Royal) Regiment of Foot	52
3rd (or the East Kent) Regiment of Foot	20	4th / 7th Royal Dragoon Guards	90
3rd (Prince of Wales's) Dragoon Guards	112	4th Dragoons	83
3rd / 4th County of London Yeomanry (Sharpshooters)	50	4th East Anglian Brigade (1908-1914)	139
		4th Horse (Irish Establishment)	90
3rd / 6th Dragoon Guards	112	4th Prince of Wales's Own Gurkha Rifles	39
3rd and 5th Dragoon Guards	25	4th Queen's Own Dragoons	83
3rd Carabiniers (Prince of Wales's Dragoon Guards)	112	4th Queen's Own Hussars	83
		4th Queen's Own Light Dragoons	83
3rd Dragoon Guards (Prince of Wales's)	112	4th Regiment of Horse (Cuirassiers)	112

Numbered Regiments and Formations	Museum Number	Numbered Regiments and Formations	Museum Number
4th Regiment of Infantry, Shah Shooja's Force (1840-1843)	39	6th or Inniskilling Regiment of Dragoons	90
4th Royal Irish Dragoon Guards	90	6th Queen Elizabeth's Own Gurkha Rifles	39
5th (or the Northumberland) Regiment of Foot	110	6th Regiment of Foot	111
		7th (Princess Royal's) Dragoon Guards	90
5th (Royal Irish) Dragoons	84	7th (Queen's Own) Light Dragoons	80
5th (Royal Irish) Lancers	84		
5th / 3rd Gurkha Rifles (1942)	39	7th (Queen's Own) Regiment of Hussars	80
5th / 6th Dragoons	90	7th Dragoon Guards (Princess Royal's)	90
5th Dragoon Guards	90		
5th Dragoon Guards (Princess Charlotte of Wales's)	90	7th Duke of Edinburgh's Own Gurkha Rifles	39
		7th Gurkha Rifles (1903-1907)	39
5th Horse	90		
5th Inniskilling Dragoon Guards	90	7th Queen's Own Hussars	80
		7th Queen's Own Regiment of Dragoons	80
5th Princess Charlotte of Wales's) Dragoon Guards	90	7th Regiment of Foot (or the Royal Fuzileers)	109
5th Regiment of Foot	110	8th (King's Royal Irish) Hussars	83
5th Regiment of Foot (Northumberland Fusiliers)	110	8th (or the King's) Regiment of Foot	55
5th Royal Gurkha Rifles (Frontier Force)	39	8th (The King's) Regiment of Foot (2nd Battalion)	65
5th Royal Inniskilling Dragoon Guards	90	8th Dragoons	83
		8th Gurkha Rifles	39
5th Royal Irish Lancers	84	8th Gurkha Rifles (1902-1907)	39
6th (Enniskilling) Regiment of Dragoons	90		
6th (Inniskilling) Dragoons	90	8th King's Royal Irish Light Dragoons	83
6th (Inniskilling) Regiment of Dragoons	90	8th Light Dragoons	83
		8th Royal Irish Hussars	83
6th (or 1st Warwickshire) Regiment of Foot	111	9th (or East Norfolk) Regiment of Foot	107
6th (The Royal 1st Warwickshire) Regiment of Foot	111	9th (Queen's) Lancers	7
		9th / 12th Royal Lancers (Prince of Wales's Own)	7
6th Dragoon Guards (Carabiniers)	112	9th Dragoons Wynne's Dragoons	7

Numbered Regiments and Formations	Museum Number	Numbered Regiments and Formations	Museum Number
9th Gurkha Rifles	39	12th Foot (The Suffolk Regiment) 2nd Battalion	138
9th Irish Horse	112		
9th Light Dragoons	7	12th Regiment of Foot	130
9th Queen's Royal Lancers	7	12th Royal Lancers (Prince of Wales's)	7
9th Regiment of Foot	107		
10th (or North Lincolnshire) Regiment of Foot	61	13th (1st Somersetshire) Regiment of Foot	123
		13th (or 1st Somersetshire) Regiment of Foot (light Infantry)	123
10th (Prince of Wales's Own Royal) Hussars	56		
10th (Prince of Wales's Own) Hussars	56	13th / 18th Royal Hussars (Queen Mary's Own)	2
10th (Prince of Wales's Own) Light Dragoons	56	13th Hussars	2
		13th Light Dragoons	2
10th Dragoons	56	13th or Prince Albert's Regiment of Light Infantry	123
10th Princess Mary's Own Gurkha Rifles	39		
10th Regiment of Foot	61	13th Regiment of Foot	123
10th Royal Hussars (Prince of Wales's Own)	56	14th (Buckinghamshire)(Prince of Wales's Own) Regiment of Foot	75
11th (or North Devonshire) Regiment of Foot	49		
		14th (Duchess of York's Own) Light Dragoons	3
11th (Prince Albert's Own) Hussars	56		
11th Dragoons	56	14th (King's) Hussars	3
11th Foot (2nd Battalion)	127	14th (King's) Light Dragoons	3
11th Gorkha Rifles	39		
11th Gurkha Rifles (1918-1922)	39	14th (or the Bedfordshire) Regiment of Foot	75
11th Hussars (Prince Albert's Own)	56	14th (or the Buckinghamshire) Regiment of Foot	75
11th Light Dragoons	56		
11th Regiment of Foot	49	14th / 20th King's Hussars	3
12 (Air Support) Engineer Brigade	134	14th Dragoons	3
		14th Gurkha Rifles (1943-1946)	39
12th (or East Suffolk) Regiment of Foot	130		
12th (Prince of Wales's Royal) Lancers	7	14th Hussars	3
		14th Light Dragoons	3
12th (Prince of Wales's) Light Dragoons	7	14th Regiment of Foot	75
		15th (King's) Light Dragoons	4
12th Dragoons Bowle's Dragoons	7	15th (or the Yorkshire East Riding) Regiment of Foot	75

Numbered Regiments and Formations	Museum Number	Numbered Regiments and Formations	Museum Number
15th / 19th King's Royal Hussars Collection	4	19th Hussars Bengal European Light Cavalry (Honourable East India Company)	4
15th Isle of Man Light AA Regiment	66		
15th King's Hussars	4	19th Light Dragoons (Drogheda's Horse)	4
15th Light Dragoons (Elliot's Light Horse)	4	19th Regiment of Foot	37
15th Regiment of Foot	75	19th Royal Hussars (Queen Alexandra's Own)	4
16th (or Bedfordshire) Regiment of Foot	16	20th (or East Devonshire) Regiment of Foot	108
16th (or the Buckinghamshire) Regiment of Foot	16	20th Foot 2nd Battalion	95
16th (Queen's) Light Dragoons	84	20th Hussars	3
		20th London Regiment	82
16th / 5th Queen's Royal Lancers	84	20th London Regiment (The Queen's Own)	82
16th Light Dragoons (Burgoyne's Light Horse)	84	20th Regiment of Foot	108
16th Queen's Lancers	84	21st (Empress of India's Lancers) 21st Hussars	84
16th Regiment of Foot	16	21st (Royal Scots Fusiliers) Regiment of Foot	96
17th (Duke of Cambridge's Own) Lancers	84		
17th (or Leicestershire) Regiment of Foot	101	21st Light Dragoons	84
17th / 21st Lancers	84	21st Regiment of Foot (or Royal North British Fuzileers)	96
17th Lancers	84		
17th Light Dragoons	84	22nd (or the Cheshire) Regiment of Foot	25
17th Regiment of Foot	101		
18th Light Dragoons	2	22nd Regiment of Foot	25
18th Light Dragoons	84	23rd (Royal Welch) Fusiliers Regiment of Foot	116
18th London Regiment	63		
18th Royal Hussars (Queen Mary's Own)	2	23rd Regiment of Foot (2nd Battalion)	28
19th (1st Yorkshire North Riding) (The Princess of Wales's Own)	37	24th (2nd Warwickshire) Regiment of Foot	125
		24th Regiment of Foot	125
19th (1st Yorkshire North Riding) Regiment of Foot	37	25th (Edinburgh) Regiment of Foot	53
19th (Prince of Wales's Own) Hussars	4	25th (or King's Own Borderers) Regiment of Foot	53
		25th (or the Sussex) Regiment of Foot	53

Numbered Regiments and Formations	Museum Number	Numbered Regiments and Formations	Museum Number
25th Gurkha Rifles (1942-1946)	39	34th (The Queen's Own, Royal West Kent) Anti-Aircraft Battalion, Royal Engineers, TA	82
26th (or Cameronian) Regiment of Foot	22		
26th Gurkha Rifles (1943-1946)	39	34th (The Queen's Own, Royal West Kent) Searchlight Regiment, Royal Artillery, TA	82
26th Regiment of Foot	22		
27th (or Inniskilling) Regiment of Foot	98		
28th (or North Gloucestershire) Regiment of Foot	122	34th Regiment of Foot	51
		35th (or the Dorsetshire) Regiment of Foot	83
28th Regiment of Foot	122	35th (or the Sussex) Regiment of Foot	83
29th (or Worcestershire) Regiment of Foot	137		
		35th (Royal Sussex) Regiment	83
29th Gurkha Rifles (1943-1946)	39		
		35th Regiment of Foot	83
29th Regiment of Foot	137	36th (or Herefordshire) Regiment of Foot	137
30th Foot (1st Cambridgeshire Regiment)	78		
		36th Foot (The Herefordshire) Regiment	40
30th Regiment of Foot	78		
31 Squadron RAF	57	36th Regiment of Foot	137
31st (Huntingdonshire) Regiment	85	37th (or the North Hampshire) Regiment of Foot	95
31st (or Huntingdonshire) Regiment of Foot	85		
		37th Regiment of Foot	95
31st Regiment of Foot	85	38th (or 1st Staffordshire) Regiment of Foot	127
32nd (Cornwall) Light Infantry	26		
		38th Gurkha Rifles (1943-1946)	39
32nd (or the Cornwall) Regiment of Foot	26		
		38th Regiment of Foot	127
33 Indian Brigade (1944)	57	39 Engineer Regiment, Royal Engineers	134
33rd (Duke of Wellington's Regiment)	27		
		39th (or Dorsetshire) Regiment of Foot	49
33rd (or 1st Yorkshire West Riding) Regiment of Foot	27		
		39th (or East Middlesex) Regiment of Foot	49
33rd Regiment of Foot	27		
34 (Air Support) Field Squadron Royal Engineers	134	39th Regiment of Foot	49
		40th (2nd Somersetshire) Regiment of Foot	78
34 Squadron RAF	57		
34th (or the Cumberland) Regiment of Foot	51	40th Regiment of Foot	78
		41st (Royal Invalids) Regiment	135

Numbered Regiments and Formations	Museum Number	Numbered Regiments and Formations	Museum Number
41st (The Welsh) Regiment of Foot	135	47th (or The Lancashire) Regiment of Foot	78
41st Regiment of Foot, or Invalids	135	47th Regiment of Foot	78
42nd (Royal Highland) Regiment of Foot 2nd Battalion	18	48 (Air Support) Field Squadron Royal Engineers	134
		48 Squadron RAF	134
42nd (The Royal Highland) Regiment of Foot	18	48th (or the Northamptonshire) Regiment of Foot	72
42nd Company Imperial Yeomanry (1900-1901)	139	48th Regiment of Foot	72
42nd Regiment of Foot	18	49th (6th or Cotterell's Marines)	92
42nd Royal Highland Regiment of Foot (The Black Watch)	18	49th (Herrfordshire) Regiment of Foot	92
43rd (Monmouthshire Light Infantry) Regiment of Foot	73	49th Princess of Wales's Herefordshire Regiment of Foot	92
43rd (Monmouthshire Light Infantry) Regiment of Foot	93	50th (or The Duke of Clarence's) Regiment of Foot	82
43rd (or the Monmouthshire) Regiment of Foot	73, 93	50th (or West Kent Regiment) of Foot	82
43rd (or the Monmouthshire) Regiment of Foot (Light Infantry)	73, 93	50th (Queen's Own) Regiment	82
		50th or The Queen's Regiment of Foot	82
43rd Regiment of Foot	73, 93	50th Regiment of Foot (December 1756)	82
44th (or the East Essex) Regiment of Foot	30	51st (2nd Yorkshire, West Riding) Regiment of Foot	54
44th Regiment of Foot	30	51st (2nd Yorkshire, West Riding) Regiment of Foot (Light Infantry)	54
45th (1st Nottinghamshire Regiment)	119		
45th (Nottinghamshire Regiment) Sherwood Foresters	119	51st (2nd Yorkshire, West Riding) The King's Own Light Infantry Regiment	54
45th Regiment of Foot	119	51st Brudenell's Regiment of Foot	54
46th (or South Devonshire) Regiment of Foot	26	51st Highland Volunteers	79
46th (South Devonshire) Regiment of Foot	26	52nd (Oxfordshire Light Infantry) Regiment	73, 93
46th Regiment of Foot	26	52nd (Oxfordshire) Regiment of Foot	73, 93

Numbered Regiments and Formations	Museum Number	Numbered Regiments and Formations	Museum Number
52nd Regiment of Foot	73	60th or The Duke of York's Own Rifle Corps	93
52nd Regiment of Foot (January 1756)	82	60th or The King's Royal Rifle Corps Regiment of Foot	93
53 (Air Support) Field Squadron Royal Engineers	134	61st (or South Gloucestershire) Regiment of Foot	122
53rd (or the Shropshire) Regiment of Foot (53rd Foot)	121	61st Regiment of Foot	122
53rd Napier's Regiment of Foot	54	62nd (Wiltshire) Regiment of Foot	92
53rd Regiment of Foot	121	62nd or The Royal American Regiment of Foot (renumbered 60th Foot)	93
54th (or West Norfolk) Regiment of Foot	49		
54th Foot raised by John Campbell (Lt Col), Duke of Argyll	49		
54th Regiment of Foot	49, 73	62nd Regiment of Foot	92
55th (or the Westmoreland) Regiment of Foot	51	63rd (or the West Suffolk) Regiment of Foot	65
55th Regiment of Foot	51	63rd Regiment of Foot (Colonel Robert Armiger)	65
56th (or the West Essex) Regiment of Foot	30	64th (or 2nd Staffordshire) Regiment of Foot	127
56th Gurkha Rifles (1943-1946)	39	64th Regiment of Foot	127
56th Regiment of Foot	30, 49	65th (2nd Yorkshire, North Riding) Regiment of Foot	138
57th (or the West Middlesex) Regiment of Foot	70	65th Regiment of Foot	138
		66th (Berkshire) Regiment of Foot	92
57th Regiment of Foot (Colonel George Perry)	51	66th Regiment of Foot	92
		67th (or South Hampshire) Regiment of Foot	95
58th (or the Rutlandshire) Regiment of Foot	72	67th Regiment of Foot	95
58th (Rutlandshire) Regiment	118	68th (or the Durham) Regiment of Foot	28
58th Regiment of Foot	30, 72	68th Regiment of Foot	28
59th (2nd Nottinghamshire) Regiment of Foot	78	69th (South Lincolnshire) Regiment of Foot	135
59th Regiment of Foot	70, 78	70th (or The Glasgow Lowland) Regiment of Foot	85
60th (Royal American) Regiment of Foot	93		
60th Foot - Raised by Colonel Robert Anstruther	72	70th (or The Surrey) Regiment of Foot	85
		70th (Surrey) Regiment	85

Numbered Regiments and Formations	Museum Number	Numbered Regiments and Formations	Museum Number
70th Regiment of Foot	85	76th (Macdonald's Highlanders) Regiment of Foot (disbanded)	27
71st (Glasgow Highland) Regiment of Foot	96		
71st (Glasgow Highland) Regiment of Foot (Light Infantry)	96	76th Regiment of Foot	27
		76th Regiment of Foot (disbanded)	27
71st (Highland Light Infantry)	96	77th (The East Middlesex) Regiment (Duke of Cambridge's Own)	70
71st (Highland) Regiment of Foot	96		
71st (Highland) Regiment of Foot (Light Infantry)	96	77th Regiment of Foot	70
72nd (Highland) Regiment of Foot	79	78th (Highland) Regiment of Foot	79
72nd (or The Duke of Albany's Own Highlanders) Regiment of Foot	79	78th (Highland) Regiment of Foot (or the Ross-Shire Buffs)	79
		78th Regiment of (Highland) Foot	79
72nd Regiment of Foot	79	79th (Herts Yeomanry) Heavy Anti-Aircraft Regiment (1938-1945)	139
73rd (Highland) Regiment of Foot	18		
73rd (Highland) Regiment of Foot - MacLeod's Highlanders	96	79th Queen's Own Cameron Highlanders	79
		79th Regiment of Foot (or Cameron Highlanders)	79
73rd (Perthshire) Regiment of Foot	18	79th Regiment of Foot (or Cameronian Highlanders)	79
73rd Regiment of Foot	18	79th Regiment of Foot (or Cameronian Volunteers)	79
74th (Highland) Regiment of Foot	96		
74th (Highland) Regiment of Foot - The Assaye Regiment	96	80th (Light-armed) Regiment of Foot (disbanded)	127
		80th (or Staffordshire Volunteers) Regiment of Foot	127
74th (Highlanders) Regiment of Foot	96		
74th Regiment of Foot	96	80th (Royal Edinburgh Volunteers) Regiment of Foot (disbanded)	127
75th (Highland) Regiment of Foot (Abercromby's Highlanders)	36		
		81st (Loyal Lincoln Volunteer) Regiment of Foot	78
75th (Stirlingshire) Regiment of Foot	36		
75th Regiment of Foot	36	81st Regiment of Foot	78
76th (Hindoostan) Regiment of Foot	27		

Numbered Regiments and Formations	Museum Number	Numbered Regiments and Formations	Museum Number
82nd Regiment of Foot (or Prince of Wales's Volunteers) Regiment of Foot	78	86th Regiment of Foot (The Shropshire Volunteers	115
83rd (County of Dublin) Regiment of Foot	115	87th (or Prince of Wales's Irish) Regiment of Foot	99
83rd Regiment of Foot (Fitch's Grenadiers)	115	87th (or Prince of Wales's Own Irish) Regiment of Foot	99
84 Squadron RAF	57	87th (or Royal Irish Fusiliers) Regiment of Foot	99
84th (York and Lancaster) Regiment of Foot	138		
84th Regiment of Foot	138	87th (Prince of Wales's Own Irish Fusiliers) Regiment of Foot	99
84th Royal Highland Emigrants Corps	138		
85th (Bucks Volunteers) (Duke of York's Own Light Infantry) Regiment	121	89th (Princess Victoria's) Regiment of Foot	99
		89th Regiment of Foot	99
85th (Bucks Volunteers) (Light Infantry) Regiment	121	90th Light Infantry Regiment, Perthshire Volunteers	22
85th (Bucks Volunteers) (The King's Light Infantry)	121	90th Perthshire Light Infantry	22
85th (Bucks Volunteers) Regiment of Foot	121	90th Regiment of Foot (or Perthshire Volunteers)	22
85th (Westminster Volunteers) Regiment of Foot	121	91st (Argyllshire Highlanders) Regiment of Foot	11
85th King's Light Infantry (85th Foot)	121	91st (Argyllshire) Regiment of Foot	11
85th Light Infantry Regiment or Royal Volunteers	121	91st (Argyllshire) Regiment of Foot (Highlanders)	11
86 (East Anglian) (Herts Yeomanry) Artillery Brigade (1920-1924)	139	91st (Princess Louise's Argyllshire Highlanders) Regiment of Foot	11
86 (East Anglian) (Herts Yeomanry) Field Artillery Brigade / Regiment (1924-1946)	139	91st Regiment of Foot	11
		92nd (Gordon Highlanders) Regiment of Foot	36
		92nd (Highland) Regiment of Foot	36
86th (Royal County Down) Regiment of Foot	115	93rd (Highland) Regiment of Foot	11

Numbered Regiments and Formations	Museum Number	Numbered Regiments and Formations	Museum Number
93rd (Sutherland Highlanders) Regiment of Foot	11	101st (Northumbrian) Regiment RA (V)	1
94 Field Regiment Royal Artillery	49	105th Madras Light Infantry	54
95th (Derbyshire) Regiment	7, 119	106th Bombay Light Infantry	28
95th (Derbyshire) Regiment of Foot	119	107th Bengal Infantry Regiment	83
95th (Rifle Regiment) (removed from numbered regiments of the line)	93	108th (Madras Infantry) Regiment of Foot	98
		108th (NH) Anti-Tank Regiment, RA	4
95th Regiment of Foot	119	135 (East Anglian) (Herts Yeomanry) Field Artillery Regiment (1939-1946)	139
96th (British Musketeers) Regiment	65	
96th (Queen's Own) Regiment of Foot	65	153 (Gurkha) Parachute Battalion (1941-1947)	39
96th (The Queen's Royal Irish) Regiment	65	154 (Gurkha) Parachute Battalion (1943-1946)	39
96th Regiment of Foot	65	191 (Herts & Essex) Yeomanry) Artillery Field Regiment (1942-1944)	139
96th Regiment of Foot (Raised as 2nd Battalion 52nd Foot)	65	
97th (Earl of Ulster's) Regiment of Foot	82	201 (Herts & Beds Yeomanry) Artillery Battery (1967-)	139
97th Regiment of Foot	82	246 Heavy Anti-Aircraft Battery (1938-1945)	139
98th (Argyllshire) Regiment of Foot (Highlanders)	11	247 Heavy Anti-Aircraft Battery (1938-1945)	139
98th (Prince of Wales's) Regiment of Foot	127	248 Heavy Anti-Aircraft Battery (1938-1945)	139
98th Regiment of Foot	127	270 Artillery Brigades (1916-1920)	139
99th (Jamaica) Regiment of Foot (disbanded)	92	273 Artillery Brigades (1916-1920)	139
99th (Lanarkshire) Regiment of Foot	92	274th (NH) Light Anti-Aircraft Battery RA Queen's Own Yeomanry	4
99th (The Duke of Edinburgh's) Regiment of Foot	92	
100th (Gordon Highlanders) Regiment of Foot	36	286 (Herts & Beds Yeomanry) Artillery Field Regiment (1961-1967)	139

Numbered Regiments and Formations	Museum Number
286 (Herts Yeomanry) Artillery Field Regiment (1956-1961)	139
286 (Herts Yeomanry) Field Artillery Regiment (1947-1954)	139
286 (Herts Yeomanry) Medium Artillery Regiment (1954-1956)	139
334 Anti-Aircraft Company Royal Engineers became 334 Searchlight Battery Royal Artillery (1937-1945)	139
336 Field Artillery Battery (1938-1946)	139
341 Artillery Battery (1920-1924)	139
341 Field Artillery Battery (1938-1946)	139
342 Artillery Battery (1920-1924)	139
342 Field Artillery Battery (1938-1946)	139
343 Artillery Battery (1920-1924)	139
343 Field Artillery Battery (1938-1946)	139
344 Artillery Battery (1920-1924)	139
344 Field Artillery Battery (1938-1946)	139
348 Artillery Brigades (1916-1920)	139
398 Heavy Anti-Aircraft Battery (1938-1945)	139
437 Heavy Anti-Aircraft Battery (1938-1945)	139
462 Field Artillery Battery (1938-1946)	139
499 Field Artillery Battery (1938-1946)	139
514 Squadron RAF	134
532 Field Artillery Battery (1942-1944)	139
533 Field Artillery Battery (1942-1944)	139
534 Field Artillery Battery (1942-1944)	139
569 (The Queen's Own) (M) LAA/SL Regiment RA TA	82
569 Searchlight Regiment RA (QORWK) TA	82
710th Gurkha Rifles (1943-1946)	39
1800 Experimental Corps of Riflemen or Rifle Corps	93

Named Regiments and Formations	Museum Number
Adjutant General's Corps	8
Air Elements of Arms and Services	69
Airborne Forces	9
Aldershot Garrison	10
Alexandra, Princess of Wales's Own Regiment of Yorkshire	37
Angus's (Earl of) Regiment of Foot	22
Argyll and Sutherland Highlanders	11
Argyll and Sutherland Highlanders (Princess Louise's)	11
Argyll's Regiment of Royal Scotsmen	38
Army Air Corps	69
Army Catering Corps	102
Army Chaplains' Department	68
Army Educational Corps	8
Army Gymnastic Staff	13

Named Regiments and Formations	Museum Number	Named Regiments and Formations	Museum Number
Army Hospital Corps	12	Bedfordshire and Hertfordshire Regiment	16
Army Legal Corps	8		
Army Legal Staff	8	Bedfordshire Regiment	16
Army Medical Department	12	Bedfordshire Yeomanry and Artillery	70
Army Medical Services	12	Bengal European Cavalry (Honourable East India Company)	84
Army Nursing Service	12		
Army Ordnance Corps	102		
Army Ordnance Department	102	Berkshire and Westminster Dragoons	17
Army Pay Corps	8	Black Watch	18
Army Pay Department	8	Black Watch (Royal Highland Regiment)	18
Army Physical Training Corps	13		
Army Physical Training Staff	13	Blues and Royals (Royal Horse Guards and 1st Dragoons)	44
Army Service Corps	102	Border Regiment	51
Army Veterinary Corps	12	Border Regiment 34th (Cumberland) Regiment of Foot	51
Arran's (Earl of) or 6th Horse	90		
Arran's Horse	90	Boys Company (1948-1968)	39
Artillery of the Honourable East India Company	33	Brecknockshire Volunteer Regiments	125
Artist's Rifles	9	Brown's (John) Horse	90
Assam Rifles	39	Buckinghamshire Home Guard	19
Auxiliary Military Pioneer Corps	102	Buckinghamshire Rifle Volunteers	19
Auxiliary Training Service	8		
Auxiliary Training Service	70	Buckinghamshire Territorial Force and Territorial Army Battalions	19
Ayrshire (Earl of Carrick's Own) Yeomanry	14		
Ayrshire Yeomanry	14	Buckinghamshire Units	19
Bank of England Volunteers	15	Buckinghamshire Volunteer Training Corps	19
Barrymore's (Earl of) Regiment of Foot (Pearce's Dragoons)	123	Buffs (East Kent Regiment)	20
Bath's (Earl of) Regiment of Foot	61	Buffs (Royal East Kent Regiment)	20
Beauclerk's Regiment	37	Burma Frontier Force (1886-1948)	39
Beaufort's (Duke of) Musketeers	49		

Named Regiments and Formations	Museum Number	Named Regiments and Formations	Museum Number
Burma Military Police (1886-1948)	39	Commissariat and Transport Corps	102
Burma Regiment (1886-1948)	39	Commissariat and Transport Department	102
Burma Rifles (1915-1942)	39	Commissariat Department	102
Cadogan's Dragoons	90	Control Department	102
Cadogan's Horse	90	Conyngham's Dragoons	90
Cambridgeshire Regiment [13]	21, 86	Coote's (Colonel Richard) Regiment of Foot	49
Cameronians (Scottish Rifles)	22	Cornwall's (Colonel Henry) Regiment of Foot	107
Carabiniers (6th Dragoon Guards)	112	Cornwall's (Duke of) Light Infantry	26
Carmarthen Militia and Volunteers	23	Corps of Armourer-Sergeants	102
Castlemartin Yeomanry	24	Corps of Army Music	105
Castleton's (Lord) Regiment of Foot	78	Corps of Army Schoolmasters	8
Charlemont's (Viscount) Regiment of Foot	137	Corps of Engineers	91
		Corps of Military Police	104
Cheshire Regiment (22nd Foot)	25	Corps of Royal Electrical and Mechanical Engineers	87
Cheshire Yeomanry	25	Corps of Royal Engineers	91
Chirbury's[14] [Cherbury's] (Lord Herbert of) Regiment of Foot	116	Corps of Royal Military Artificers	91
		Corps of Royal Military Police	104
Cholmondeleley's (Colonel) Regiment of Foot	72	Corps of Royal Military Police and Military Provost Staff Corps	8
Churchill's Dragoons	56	Corps of Royal Sappers and Miners	91
Churchill's Marines	85		
Clifton's (Sir William) Regiment of Foot	75	Corps of Waggoners	102
Cobham's Dragoons	56	Coy's Horse (6th Horse)	90
Cobham's Horse	90	Crauford's Regiment of Foot	121
Coldstream Guards	38	Crawford's (Earl of) Regiment of Foot (The Highland Regiment)	18
Coldstream Regiment of Foot Guards	38		
		Cumberland & Westmoreland Rifle Volunteers	51
		Cumberland Artillery	51

---

[13] Also see the Imperial War Museum, Duxford

[14] Two spellings of the surname are given namely, Lord Herbert Chirbury and Lord Herbert Cherbury. It is believed that both were used historically.

Named Regiments and Formations	Museum Number	Named Regiments and Formations	Museum Number
Cumberland Militia	51	East Lancashire Regiment	78
Cunningham's Dragoons	80	East Riding of Yorkshire	29
Dalrymple's or Stair's Dragoons	90	Yeomanry	
		East Surrey Regiment	85
Davenport's Horse (Prince of Wales's Own Regiment of Horse)	90	East Yorks Militia	6
		East Yorks Rifle Volunteers	6
De Jean's Regiment of Foot	95	East Yorkshire Regiment	75
Denbighshire Hussars Yeomanry	116	East Yorkshire Regiment (Duke of York's Own)	75
Deptford Volunteers	82	East Yorkshire Regiment 4th Battalion	6
Derbyshire Regiment (Sherwood Foresters)	119	Eastern or Rungpore Battalion (1815-1830)	39
Derbyshire Yeomanry	7	Eaton Hall Officer Cadet School (National Service)	25
Dering's (Sir Edward) Regiment of Foot	125	Echlin's Dragoons	90
Devonshire and Dorset Regiment	49	Edinburgh's (Duke of) Royal Regiment (Berkshire and Wiltshire)	92
Devonshire Regiment	49		
Devonshire's (Earl of) or 10th Horse	90	Erle's Regiment	37
Donegal's (Earl of) Regiment of Foot - The Belfast Regiment	83	Essex & Suffolk Royal Garrison Artillery	30
		Essex (Fortress) Royal Engineers	30
Dorset Militia	49	Essex Artillery Volunteers	30
Dorset Regiment	49	Essex Home Guard	30
Dorset Yeomanry	49	Essex Local Defence Volunteers	30
Douglas's (Colonel) Regiment of Foot	16	Essex Militia, Rifles, Rifle Volunteer and Volunteer units	30
Duke of Lancaster's Own Yeomanry	3		
Dumbarton's (Earl of) Regiment (1st Foot)	113	Essex Regiment	30
		Essex Yeomanry	31
Durham Light Infantry	28	Essex Yeomanry Cavalry	30
Durham Militia, Rifle Volunteers and Durham Home Guard	28	Eyre Coote's 84th Regiment of Foot	138
		Fane's Regiment of Foot	95
East Anglian Artillery Brigade 1st/4th, 2nd/4th, 3rd/4th (1914-1916)	139	Farrington's (Colonel) Regiment of Foot	137
		Fielding's (Colonel) Regiment of Foot	135
East India Company Engineer Corps	91	Fife and Forfar Yeomanry	32

Named Regiments and Formations	Museum Number	Named Regiments and Formations	Museum Number
Fowke's (Colonel) Regiment of Foot (54th Foot) (renumbered 43rd Foot)	73, 93	Gurkha Independent Parachute Company (1961-1971)	39
Fox's (Colonel) Regiment of Marines (disbanded and re-raised as 32nd Foot)	26	Gurkha Military Police (1949-1970)	39
Fusiliers' London Volunteers	34	Hales's (Sir Edward) Regiment of Foot	75
General's (Lord) Regiment of Foot	38	Hamilton's Horse	90
General's (Lord) Regiment of Foot Guards	38	Hampshire Regiment	95
Gentlemen Cadet Registers	103	Hampshire Regiment (The), 11th (Royal Militia of Jersey) Battalion	95
Gibson's (Colonel) Regiment of Foot	122	Hampshire Regiment (The), 6th (Duke of Connaught's Own) Battalion	95
Glamorgan Artillery Volunteers	35	Hampshire Regiment (The), 8th (Princess Beatrice's Own Isle of Wight Rifles) Battalion	95
Glasgow Greys	85		
Glasgow Highlanders (9th Battalion Highland Light Infantry)	96	Harwich's or 8th Horse	90
Glider Pilot Regiment	9, 69	Herbert's Regiment	116
Gloucestershire Regiment	122	Herefordshire Light Infantry	40
Godfrey's Horse	90	Herefordshire Regiment	40
Gorakhpore Hill Rangers (1815-1816)	39	Herefordshire Rifle Volunteer Corps	40
Gordon Highlanders	36	Hertfordshire Imperial Yeomanry (1901-1908)	139
Gore's Dragoons	56	Hertfordshire Regiment	41
Goring's Marines	85	Hertfordshire Troops of Yeomanry and Volunteer Cavalry (1794-1821)	139
Gray's Regiment of Foot	95		
Green Howards	37	Hertfordshire Yeomanry and Artillery	42
Green Howards (Alexandra, Princess of Wales's Own Yorkshire Regiment)	37	Hertfordshire Yeomanry Cavalry (1871-1901)	139
Grenadier Guards	38	Hertfordshire Yeomanry Cavalry (Northern, Dacorum & Gilston Troops) (1830-1871)	139
Guards Camel Regiment	38		
Guards Machine Gun Regiment	38		
Guards Parachute Company	38		

Named Regiments and Formations	Museum Number	Named Regiments and Formations	Museum Number
Hertfordshire Yeomanry, Territorial Force (1908-1920)	139	Kent and Sharpshooters Yeomanry	50
		Kent Cyclist Battalions	82
Herts Artillery Batteries 1st/1st, 2nd/1st, 1st/2nd, 2nd/2nd (1914-1916)	139	Kerr's Dragoons	56
		Ker's Dragoons	80
Highland Light Infantry	96	King's (Liverpool Regiment)	55
Highlanders (The) , (Seaforth Gordons and Camerons)	36, 79	King's (Shropshire Light Infantry)	121
Hinchinbroke's Regiment of Foot	95	King's Light Infantry (Shropshire Regiment)	121
His Majesty's Regiment of Guards	38	King's Own (Royal Lancaster Regiment)	52
His Majesty's Regiment of Guards (Wentworth's Regiment)	38	King's Own (Royal Lancaster) Regiment	52
		King's Own Borderers	53
Honeywood's Dragoons	56	King's Own Regiment of Foot	52
Honourable Artillery Company	43	King's Own Royal Regiment (Lancaster)	52
Horse Grenadier Guards	44	King's Own Scottish Borderers	53
Horse Guards	44	King's Regiment (Liverpool)	55
Household Cavalry	44	King's Regiment (Manchester and Liverpool)	55
Howard's Regiment	37		
Huntingdon's (Earl of) Regiment of Foot	27, 123		
Huske's Regiment	116	King's Regiment of Foot	55
Indian Engineers including Bengal, Bombay and Madras Groups	91	King's Royal Rifle Corps	93
		King's (The) , (Liverpool Regiment), 8th (Scottish) Volunteer Battalion	62
Infantry Weapons	45		
Ingoldsby's Regiment	116	King's (The) Foot Guards	38
Inniskilling (6th Dragoons)	90	King's (The) Lyfe Guards of Foot	38
Inns of Court and City Yeomanry	46		
Intelligence Corps	47	King's (The) Regiment	38
Irish Guards	38	King's (The), (Liverpool Regiment) Territorial Force, 10th (Scottish) Battalion	62
Jammu and Kashmir Units	39		
Jedburgh's Dragoons	80		
Jersey Militia	48		
Jocelyn's Horse	90	King's or 1st Regiment of Horse	44
Kellum's Horse	90		
		King's Own Militia	19

Named Regiments and Formations	Museum Number	Named Regiments and Formations	Museum Number
King's Own Royal Border Regiment	51, 52	Life Guards	44
King's Own Yorkshire Light Infantry	54	Life Guards (1st and 2nd)	44
		Light Dragoons	2, 4
King's Regiment	55, 65	Light Infantry	26, 28, 54, 60, 121, 123
King's Regiment of Horse, 2nd Horse	5		
King's Royal Hussars	3, 56	Ligonier's or 8th Horse	90
King's Royal Regiment of Guards	38	Lillingston's (Colonel) Regiment of Foot	111
King's Shropshire Light Infantry	121	Lillington's (Colonel) Regiment of Foot	127
Kohima Garrison (1944)	57	Lincolnshire Regiment	61
Labour Corps	102	Lincolnshire Yeomanry	61
Lambton's (Colonel) Regiment of Foot (54th Foot) (renumbered 52nd Foot)	93	Liverpool Scottish	79
		Liverpool Scottish Queen's Own Cameron Highlanders (TA)	62
Lanarkshire Volunteer, Militia and Yeomanry units	22	Liverpool Scottish Regiment	62
		London Irish Rifles	63
Lancashire Fusiliers	108	London Regiment (The), 20th (County of London) Battalion	82
Lancashire Regiment	3		
Lancashire Regiment (Prince of Wales's Volunteers)	78	London Scottish (The), (The Gordon Highlanders)	36
Land Transport Corps	102	London Scottish Regiment	64
Langdale's Horse	90	Long's (Colonel) Regiment of Foot	30
Langston's Horse	90	Lothian Regiment (Royal Scots)	113
Le Régiment d'Hébron	113		
Le Régiment de Douglas	113	Lovat Scouts	79
Leeds Rifles	58	Loyal Greenwich Volunteer Infantry	82
Leicestershire Regiment	101		
Leicestershire Rifle Volunteers	118	Loyal Greenwich Water Fencibles	82
Leicestershire Yeomanry	59, 118	Loyal Lincolnshire Volunteers Regiment of Foot	78
Leinster's or 8th Horse	90		
Leslie's or Rothe's Dragoons	90	Loyal North Lancashire Regiment	78
Leven's (Earl of) Regiment of Foot (The Edinburgh Regiment)	53	Loyal Regiment (North Lancashire)	78
Leveson's Dragoons	80		

Named Regiments and Formations	Museum Number	Named Regiments and Formations	Museum Number
Lucas's (Lord) Regiment of Foot	51	Munro's Regiment of Foot	95
Luttrell's (Colonel) Companies of Foot	37	Murray's Regiment of Foot	95
Luttrell's Marines	85	Napier's Horse	90
Machine Gun Guards	38	Neville's Horse	90
Manchester Regiment	65	New Regiment of Foot Guards	38
Manx Regiment	66	Norfolk Regiment	107
Mar's (The Earl of) Regiment of Foot	96	Norfolk's (Duke of) Regiment of Foot	25, 130
Medical Staff Corps	12	North British Fusiliers (Fuzileers)	96
Meredith's Regiment of Foot	95	North Devon Yeomanry Hussars	89
Middlesex Regiment	70	North Irish Horse	71
Military Foot Police	104	North Riding Rifle Volunteer Corps	37
Military Mounted Police	104	North Somerset Yeomanry Collection	123
Military Prison Staff Corps	104		
Military Provost Staff Corps	104	North Yorkshire Light Infantry Regiment of Militia	37
Military Store Staff Corps	102		
Military Stores Department	102	North Yorkshire Regiment of Militia	37
Military Survey	91	North Yorkshire Rifles (Militia)	37
Military Train	102		
Monck's (General) Regiment (The Coldstreamers)	38	Northamptonshire Regiment	72
Monmouthshire Militia	125	Northamptonshire Yeomanry	72
Monmouthshire Regiment Collection	125	Northumberland & Newcastle Volunteer Cavalry Imperial Yeomanry (1900-1902)	4
Montgomeryshire Hussars Yeomanry	116		
Montgomeryshire Volunteer Regiment	125	Northumberland Fusiliers	110
Montgomeryshire Yeomanry	67	Northumberland Hussars	4
Mordaunt (Henry), Earl of Peterborough - The Tangier Regiment	85	Nusseree Battalion (1850-1861)	39
		O'Brien's (Lord) Regiment (or the Irish Regiment)	110
Mordaunt's (Colonel) Regiment of Foot	78	Ordnance Store Branch	102
Morgan's Regiment	116	Ordnance Store Corps	102

Named Regiments and Formations	Museum Number	Named Regiments and Formations	Museum Number
Ordnance Store Department	102	Prince of Wales's Own Royal Regiment of Welsh Fuzileers	116
Our Regiment of Guards	38		
Oxfordshire and Buckinghamshire Light Infantry	73, 93	Princess Anne of Denmark's Regiment of Foot	55
Parachute Regiment	9	Princess Anne of Denmark's Regiment of Dragoons	83
Pearce's Horse	90		
Peer's Regiment	116		
Pembrokeshire Yeomanry	74	Princess Charlotte of Wales's Berkshire Regiment	92
Peyton's (Colonel Sir Robert) Companies of Foot	108		
		Princess Louise's (Argyll and Sutherland Highlanders)	11
Phillips's (Colonel) Regiment of Foot	78		
Pioneer Corps	102	Princess Louise's Kensington Regiment	76
Plymouth's (Earl of) Regiment for Tangier (2nd Tangier Regiment)	52	Princess of Wales's Own (Yorkshire Regiment)	37
Polwarth's Dragoons	80	Princess of Wales's Own Regiment of Foot	85
Ponsonby's Regiment of Foot	95	Princess of Wales's Own (Yorkshire Regiment) Militia	37
Price's (Colonel) Regiment of Foot	26		
Prince Albert's (Somerset Light Infantry)	123	Princess of Wales's Own Royal Regiment of Dragoons	80
Prince Albert's (Somersetshire Light Infantry)	123	Princess of Wales's Own Royal Regiment of Horse	5
Prince Consort's Own Rifle Brigade	93	Princess of Wales's Own Yorkshire Regiment Territorial Battalions	37
Prince George of Denmark's Regiment of Foot	20	Princess of Wales's Own Yorkshire Regiment Volunteer Battalions	37
Prince of Wales's (North Staffordshire Regiment)	127		
		Princess of Wales's Royal Regiment (Queen's and Royal Hampshires)	20, 77, 85, 95
Prince of Wales's Own (West Yorkshire Regiment)	75		
		Princess Victoria's (Royal Irish Fusiliers)	99
Prince of Wales's Own Regiment of Yorkshire	75	Purcell's Regiment	116

Named Regiments and Formations	Museum Number	Named Regiments and Formations	Museum Number
Q (The Queen's Own) Battery, 265 LAA Regiment RA TA	82	Queen's Own Buffs, Royal Kent Regiment	20
Queen Alexandra's Royal Army Nursing Corps	12	Queen's Own Cameron Highlanders	79
Queen Alexandra's Imperial Military Nursing Service	12	Queen's Own Dorset Yeomanry	49
Queen Consort's Own Regiment of Dragoons	80	Queen's Own Gurkha Transport Regiment	39
Queen Consort's Regiment	52	Queen's Own Highlanders (Seaforth and Camerons)	79
Queen Dowager's Regiment	85	Queen's Own Hussars	80
Queen Dowager's Royal Regiment	85	Queen's Own Mercian Yeomanry	81, 121
Queen's (Royal West Surrey) Regiment	85	Queen's Own Royal Regiment of Dragoons	80
Queen's Own (Royal West Kent Regiment)	82	Queen's Own Royal Regiment of Foot	85
Queen's Own Regiment of Foot	52	Queen's Own Royal Regiment of Horse	5
Queen's Regiment of Foot (or Webb's Regiment)	55	Queen's Own Royal West Kent Regiment	82
Queen's Royal Regiment	85	Queen's Own Royal West Kent Regiment (The), 6th (Cyclist) Battalion	82
Queen's Royal Regiment (West Surrey)	85	Queen's Own West Kent Yeomanry	50
Queen's	85	Queen's Regiment	52, 77, 85
Queen's (Second) Royal Regiment of Foot	85	Queen's Regiment (Middlesex) 4th Battalion	77
Queen's (The)	85	Queen's Regiment (Queen's Own Buffs) 2nd Battalion	77
Queen's Gurkha Engineers	39		
Queen's Gurkha Signals	39	Queen's Regiment (Queen's Surreys) 1st Battalion	77
Queen's Lancashire Regiment	78		
Queen's Marines (By Colonel's Names 1710-1715)	52	Queen's Regiment (Royal Sussex) 3rd Battalion	77
Queen's or 2nd Regiment of Horse	5	Queen's Royal Hussars (The Queen's Own and Royal Irish)	80, 83
Queen's Own (The), (Royal West Kent Regiment), 2nd Volunteer Battalion	82	Queen's Royal Irish Hussars	83

Named Regiments and Formations	Museum Number	Named Regiments and Formations	Museum Number
Queen's Royal Lancers	84	Royal Cumberland Militia	51
Queen's Royal Surrey Regiment	85	Royal Devon Yeomanry	89
		Royal Dorset Yeomanry	49
Queen's Surreys	85	Royal Dragoon Guards	90
RA (TA)	66	Royal East Kent Mounted Rifle	50
Radnorshire Volunteer Regiment	125	Royal Engineers	91
Richard's (Colonel) Regiment of Foot	101	Royal Engineers Balloon Units (RAF Museum, Hendon)	91
Rifle Brigade	93	Royal Engineers Bomb Disposal	91
Rifle Brigade (Prince Consort's Own)	93	Royal Engineers Postal and Courier Services	102
Rifle Brigade (The Prince Consort's Own)	93	Royal Engineers Postal and Courier Services (Royal Logistic Corps Museum)	91
Royal 1st Devon Yeomanry	89		
Royal Anglian Regiment	30, 61, 72, 86, 101, 107, 130	Royal Engineers Signals Service	91, 114
		Royal Engineers Submarine Service	91
Royal Armoured Corps	132	Royal Engineers Telegraphs	91, 114
Royal Army Chaplains' Department	68	Royal Field Artillery	33
Royal Army Dental Corps	12	Royal Flying Corps	69
Royal Army Educational Corps	8	Royal Fusiliers	109
		Royal Fusiliers (City of London Regiment)	109
Royal Army Medical Corps	12	Royal Garrison Artillery	33
Royal Army Ordnance Corps	102	Royal Gloucestershire Hussars	122
Royal Army Pay Corps	8	Royal Gloucestershire, Berkshire and Wiltshire Regiment	92, 122
Royal Army Service Corps	102		
Royal Army Veterinary Corps	12		
Royal Artillery	33	Royal Green Jackets	73, 93
Royal Berkshire Regiment (Princess Charlotte of Wales's)	92	Royal Guernsey Light Infantry	94
		Royal Guernsey Militia	94
Royal Berkshire Yeomanry	88	Royal Gurkha Rifles	39
		Royal Hampshire Regiment	95
Royal Corps of Signals	114		
Royal Corps of Transport	102	Royal Highland Fusiliers	96

Named Regiments and Formations	Museum Number	Named Regiments and Formations	Museum Number
Royal Highland Fusiliers (Princess Margaret's Own Glasgow and Ayrshire Regiment)	96	Royal Monmouthshire Royal Engineers (Militia)	106
		Royal Norfolk Regiment	107
		Royal North British Fusiliers	96
Royal Horse Artillery	33		
Royal Horse Guards (Blue)	44	Royal North Devon Yeomanry	89
Royal Horse Guards (The Blues)	44	Royal Northumberland Fusiliers	110
Royal Hospital	97	Royal Pioneer Corps	102
Royal Hussars (Prince of Wales's Own)	56	Royal Regiment of Artillery	33
Royal Inniskilling Fusiliers	98	Royal Regiment of Foot	113
		Royal Regiment of Fusiliers	108, 109, 110, 111
Royal Irish Artillery	33		
Royal Irish Fusiliers	99	Royal Regiment of Fuzilieers (or Ordnance Regiment)	109
Royal Irish Fusiliers (Princess Victoria's)	99		
Royal Irish Rangers (27th, 83rd, 86th, 87th, 89th and 108th Foot)	100	Royal Regiment of Horse (Oxford Blues)	44
		Royal Regiment of Scots Dragoons	112
Royal Irish Regiment	98, 99, 100, 115	Royal Regiment of Wales	125, 135
Royal Irish Regiment (27th (Inniskilling), 83rd, 87th and The Ulster Defence Regiment)	100	Royal Regiment of Welsh Fuzileers	116
		Royal Scots	113
Royal Irish Rifles	115	Royal Scots (The Lothian Regiment)	113
Royal Leicestershire Regiment	86, 101	Royal Scots (The Royal Regiment)	113
Royal Lincolnshire Regiment	61	Royal Scots Dragoon Guards	112
Royal Logistic Corps	102	Royal Scots Dragoon Guards (Carabiniers and Greys)	112
Royal Military Academy Sandhurst	103		
Royal Military Academy Woolwich	103	Royal Scots Fusiliers	96
		Royal Scots Greys (2nd Dragoons)	112
Royal Military College Sandhurst	103	Royal Signals	114
Royal Monmouthshire (Light Infantry) Militia - 31st Foot	106	Royal Sussex Regiment	83
		Royal Tank Corps	132
		Royal Tank Regiment	132
		Royal Ulster Rifles	115

Named Regiments and Formations	Museum Number	Named Regiments and Formations	Museum Number
Royal Waggon Train	102	Shropshire Rifle Volunteers	121
Royal Warwickshire Fusiliers	111	Shropshire Royal Horse Artillery	121
Royal Warwickshire Regiment	111	Shropshire Yeomanry	121
Royal Welch Fusiliers	116	Small Arms School	45
Royal Welsh Fusiliers	116	Small Arms School Corps	45
Royal West Kent Regiment (Queen's Own)	82	Somerset and Cornwall Light Infantry	26, 123
Royal West Surrey Regiment (The Queen's)	85	Somerset Light Infantry	123
Royal West Surreys	85	Somerset Light Infantry (Prince Albert's)	123
Royal Westmoreland Light Infantry Militia	51	Somerset Militia	123
Royal Wiltshire Yeomanry	117	Somerset Rifle Volunteer Regiments	123
Rutland Militia	118	South Hertfordshire Yeomanry Cavalry (1830-1871)	139
Rutland Yeomanry Cavalry	118	South Lancashire Regiment (Prince of Wales's Volunteers)	78
Sabine's Regiment	116	South Nottinghamshire Hussars Yeomanry	124
Salop Militia	121	South Staffordshire Regiment	127
Sandersons' (Colonel) Regiment of Marines	78	South Wales Borderers	125
Schomberg's or 10th Horse	90	Special Air Service Regiment	9
Schomberg's or 8th Horse	90	Staff Band, Brigade of Gurkhas	39
Scotch Guards (or Scotts Guards)	38	Staff College	126
Scots Fusilier Guards	38	Staffordshire Regiment	127
Scots Guards	38	Staffordshire Regiment (Prince of Wales's)	127
Scottish Yeomanry	14	Staffordshire Yeomanry	128
Seaforth Highlanders (Ross-shire Buffs, The Duke of Albany's)	79	Stuart's Regiment of Foot	95
Selkirk's (Earl of) Horse	90	Suffolk and Norfolk Yeomanry	129
Sherwood Foresters (Derbyshire Regiment)	119	Suffolk Regiment	130
Sherwood Foresters (Nottinghamshire & Derbyshire Regiment)	119	Surrey Regiment 2nd Battalion	85
Sherwood Rangers Yeomanry	120	Sussex Yeomanry	131
Shrewsbury's or 7th Horse	90	Sutton's Regiment	37

Named Regiments and Formations	Museum Number	Named Regiments and Formations	Museum Number
Sybourg's or 8th Horse	90	Westmorland and Cumberland Yeomanry	136
Sylhet Frontier Corps (1817-1823)	39	Wills' (General) Regiment of Foot	78
Tank Corps	132	Wiltshire Regiment (Duke of Edinburgh's)	92
Territorial Army Nursing Service	12	Windress' Regiment of Foot	95
Tiffin's (Colonel Zachariah) Enniskillen Regiment of Foot	98	Women's Royal Army Corps	8, 70
Trelawney's (Colonel Edward) Regiment of Foot	92	Women's Army Auxiliary Corps	8, 70
Tyrawley's Horse	90	Worcestershire and Sherwood Foresters Regiment	119, 137
Ulster Defence Regiment	100	Worcestershire Regiment	137
'V' (The Liverpool Scottish) Company 1st Battalion 51st Highlander Volunteers	62	Worcestershire Yeomanry Collection	137
'V' (The Liverpool Scottish) Company 5th/8th (Volunteer) Battalion The King's Regiment	62	Wynne's Horse	90
		York (Duchess of) and Albany's Regiment	52
Veterinary Medical Department	12	York and Lancaster Regiment (Disbanded 1968)	138
Villiers's Regiment of Marines	85		
Warwickshire Yeomanry	133		
Welch Regiment	135		
Wellington's (Duke of) (West Riding Regiment)	27		
Welsh Guards	38		
Welsh Regiment of Fuzileers	116		
Wenteorth's Horse	90		
West Somerset Yeomanry Collection	123		
West Yorkshire Regiment (The Prince of Wales's Own)	75		
Western or Bettiah Corps (1813-1826)	39		
Westminster Dragoons	17		
Westmoreland Militia	51		

Index

127

N

O

P

134

About the Author

Dr Stuart C Blank

Dr Blank's interest in military history commenced at an early age when he was given his grandfather's World War 1 medals. This embarked him on a voyage of discovery which is still ongoing. He is a member of the Orders and Medals Research Society, the premier body in the UK, for research into numismatics.

He has been an Independent (Freelance) Researcher at some of the UK's major archive facilities for a number of years and he offers his Professional Research Services to the public. The website *www.MilitaryArchiveResearch.com* gives further details of the services that he offers. He has conducted previous research ranging from military genealogy (i.e. researching individual servicemen / women), regimental (and units') histories, to the movements of Royal and Merchant Navy shipping, chemical weapons and the history of individual Royal Air Force aircraft. This book is a culmination of his research into the material that is available on the Internet that significantly benefits the study of British military history with specific reference to the Army.

If any reader would like to see other Internet sites included in this publication or to update existing ones then please e-mail the author on enquiries@MilitaryArchiveResearch.com.

Dr Stuart C Blank
January 2007